Grace Notes

Grace
Notes

Katey Sagal

G

GALLERY BOOKS

New York   London   Toronto   Sydney   New Delhi

G

Gallery Books
An Imprint of Simon & Schuster, Inc.
1230 Avenue of the Americas
New York, NY 10020

First Gallery Books hardcover edition March 2017

GALLERY BOOKS and colophon are registered trademarks of Simon & Schuster, Inc.

For information about special discounts for bulk purchases, please contact Simon &
Schuster Special Sales at 1-866-506-1949 or business@simonandschuster.com.

The Simon & Schuster Speakers Bureau can bring authors to your live event. For more
information or to book an event, contact the Simon & Schuster Speakers Bureau at
1-866-248-3049 or visit our website at www.simonspeakers.com.

Designed by Jaime Putorti

Manufactured in the United States of America

10 9 8 7 6 5 4 3 2 1

Library of Congress Cataloging-in-Publication Data
Names: Sagal, Katey, author.
Title: Grace notes : my recollections / Katey Sagal.
Description: First Gallery Books hardcover edition. | New York : Gallery
   Books, [2017]
Identifiers: LCCN 2016039352 | ISBN 9781476796710 (hardback) | ISBN
   9781476796727 (trade paper) | ISBN 9781476796734 (ebook)
Subjects: LCSH: Sagal, Katey. | Television actors and actresses—United
   States—Biography. | Women singers—United States—Biography. | BISAC:
   BIOGRAPHY & AUTOBIOGRAPHY / Personal Memoirs. | BIOGRAPHY
   & AUTOBIOGRAPHY / Entertainment & Performing Arts. | BIOGRAPHY &
   AUTOBIOGRAPHY / Women.
Classification: LCC PN2287.S185 A3 2017 | DDC 791.4502/8092 [B] —dc23 LC
   record available at https://lccn.loc.gov/2016039352

ISBN 978-1-4767-9671-0
ISBN 978-1-4767-9673-4 (ebook)

This book is dedicated, with love,
to Sarah, Jackson, and Esmé.

❧ Contents ❧

Grace
Notes

Prologue

January 2012

I am getting older.

It's time to write shit down.

When I'm doing my best thinking, in my car,
I tell myself all the things I need to write down.

Because I am older.

I could lie before.

Knocking off years was easy, and I believed the lie.

Not so much these days.

Now it's different.

I want to tell my kids things about me that one day it might
be too late to tell them.

So they know where I started.

So they know where they started.

Without having to fill in the blanks from the dribs and drabs of distant relatives, as I have had to do.

As I am, even now, doing.

I might write it down for them, the three who think that I've given them life.

When, really, it's been the other way around.

They have given me life.

They have grown me up.

It is to them that I am indebted.

Cause time moves quick, and the teenagers aren't home for dinner as much anymore.

And the five-year-old eats at five, and that's too early for me.

The conversations feel shorter lately.

The teenagers talk above me.

The little one screams a lot.

I just really need to write it out, so I will never forget.

And so they will always know.

I need to start now.

Because getting older makes me think a lot about the end.

Actually that's not new.

I've always thought—kind of obsessively—about the end.

Having parents die young does that to a person.

I have a keen sense of my mortality.

My shrink tells me all the time that not all folks have that. Who knew?

My keen sense of knowing that this amazing life I have could end at any time is a fucking pain in my ass. Seriously.

And always on my mind.

And because every year someone in my sphere—a manager, or an agent, or a friend—tells me I should write a memoir, saying, "You've been through a lot," I began to take the idea more seriously. But I would need to do it my way, not a beginning, middle, and end recollection. These are my snippets, my musings, the moments that I think you should know. There's more, I'm sure, but I'm not dead yet.

I have just about had my fill of life's small distractions.

So it might be time.

I've shopped enough. (I think?)

Moved enough, lived in enough new houses.

I've traveled a bunch.

I've dated and married enough times.

As much as I like to watch TV, even that can't hold me the way it used to.

In other words, I have time.

Time to write.

I can sit still now.

I meditate now. (Something I never thought possible!)

Two of my three kids are close to launch.

Sarah to college this year.

The boy, Jackson, behind the wheel of a car in March.

I can see that dreamy look in his eyes as he envisions, finally, the bit of breathing room that only your own car can provide.

He cannot wait to fly solo.

The baby, just five years old, will still be the baby for a while.

But still, one kid at home compared with three feels like I'll have more time.

A psychic (feel free to judge) once told me I would have a life of high highs and low lows, but not much middle ground.

It's been true.

Until now.

I now feel more grounded in the center of myself, with no desire for overstimulation or permission needed to wallow in wherever I am.

To be myself.

My children provide significance.

So I'll do this for the three of them.

For you, Sarah, Jackson, and Esmé.

For you.

The Singing Sweetheart
of Cherokee County

When I was ten, my mother taught me to play the guitar. We were living in the Westwood section of Los Angeles at the time. Dark and cavernous, the house seemed to me an enormous Spanish hacienda. (I went back years later, and it was more like a casita.) Mom and I sat in the living room, the dark wooden floors and rich red tiles providing the effect of an echo chamber. My mom, as always, was dressed in her simple way, with her hair cut in a short, unstuffy style that I understood later was meant to avoid adding complications to her life.

"Darling girl!" She called me to her. "Let me show you. This is what I did at your age."

I sat on her lap, the guitar in mine, with her arms draped around me, and we picked and strummed in tandem, like one person. My hands hurt as I stretched and pressed my fingers into the strings. She rested her hands, bird-like and delicate, on top of mine and helped to mold my fingers into chord formations with one hand while strumming with the other. If I concentrate, I can still feel her small hands touching me. I was so much bigger than her, even as a little kid. She was happy then and suntanned, memorable because it was rare that she had color. She stayed inside so much of the time.

"Down in the Valley" was the first song I learned. A traditional folk ballad my mom played every time she picked up her guitar. We sang loudly. My hands wrapped around the wide neck of Mom's maple-colored Martin. Her nylon string acoustic guitar, the one she was given by Burl Ives. I never really knew why or how she got his guitar; that's one of the heartbreaks of having dead parents: no one to fill in the blanks.

"Down in the valley, valley so low, hang your head over, hear the wind blow . . ."

Kent cigarettes, butts and burning, in an ashtray nearby. The smell of slept-in clothes, dirty hair, and tobacco—the smells of my mom—filling the space along with the low, rich tones of her voice. A deep alto by this time in her life, she still sang with the faint twang of the yodeler she was in her younger years. Long ago, when my mother was eleven years old, she had her own fifteen-minute daily radio show out of Gaffney, South Carolina. She was known as "the Singing Sweetheart of Cherokee County."

I imagine Mom at eleven to have been hopeful and enthusiastic, full of promise and invigorated by life's possibilities. But this Mom—the Mom at age thirty-five whom I sat with in our living room—her, not so much. This was years after the radio show. Much had happened in her life—and not happened.

By the time I was old enough to know my mom, she'd moved far beyond "the Singing Sweetheart of Cherokee County" to a life of darkened rooms and hushed hallways, the house's forced stillness when she had taken to her bed. The official diagnosis was heart disease, but I've always thought she had a broken heart.

Mom had started working young and would continue to do so in many different forms until she married. From the radio show at eleven in Gaffney, she was discovered by NBC Radio and sent to New York to continue her show. The family lore goes that my gambling granddad, Daniel, had left my grandmother for the racetrack one day and never returned. And with my mom footing the bill with her radio show paychecks, my grandma moved herself and four kids to the Big Apple. My mom helped to support them all, while Grandma Virginia found a job, went back to school, and eventually landed the position of the dean of women at Hunter College.

In her early twenties, during World War II, my mom entertained the troops overseas on tour with the USO and later appeared on Broadway. At some point, she moved to the other side of the line, got a gig working for Norman Lear on *The Martin and Lewis Show* as script supervisor, and in time became the first woman assistant director in live television. She also did her share of writing.

What I remember?

Rin Tin Tin comic books and several soap operas written under an alias.

My mom had plans, and hopes; more to say and create.

However, work came to a screeching standstill when she met my dad, a Russian cab driver by day with a theater degree and an ambition to direct. She loved him. She was twenty-five years old when in 1952 she tied the knot, an age considered borderline "over the hill." And as was expected in her generation, she gave up her career and started making babies. My sense is that parenting paled in comparison with her dreams, and she was never really *at home* with her role as "Mom."

I'm the oldest of five. Soon after her second baby was born, her life became filled with bouts of depression and the occasional suicide attempt. Searching for answers, there were medications and therapists, and eventually institutions, sanitariums, and shock treatments. Maybe my mom just needed a job! I always felt she was born in the wrong generation. Things were changing slowly for women during the 1950s and 1960s, but wife and mother was still the norm, and when she tried to do what was now expected of her, it broke her heart. All of the treatments in the world couldn't make it okay. She felt silenced.

We were living in Encino, California, the first time my mom "went away," and my grandma came to stay. With three kids— me, my brothers David and Joey—under the age of five, my mom was institutionalized for depression and treated the electroshock therapy way. My workaholic dad neither asked for nor knew how to handle my mom's illness with much more than hysteria and more work.

So arrived my mom's mom, Virginia Lee Zwilling. Alabama born, ladylike and soft-spoken, a true Southern matriarch, she knew how to bring calm in the midst of crazy.

"It's gonna be aaalright, dahlin', don't you worry your pretty little head," she'd say, standing solid.

No hurdle too high.

No waters too deep.

She was unshakeable.

Virginia Lee came into our lives as the wheels were comin' off and stealthily did what needed to be done.

I have no recollection of my mom leaving for an extended stay.

There was no discussion of "vacation" or "visiting relatives."

She was just gone.

I have no memory of my grandmother moving in.

She was just there.

As if she'd always been there.

Virginia Lee picked up the pieces more than once when Mom was "away." With her chicken and dumplings and Bisquick biscuits, over the years she became my teacher of all things domestic.

Each visit, she would teach me a new household skill.

She taught me how to set a table and make bed "corners." How to sew on a button, iron and fold the laundry, get a hot meal on the table.

How to write a check.

How to mix a martini.

She knew, for me to feel safe, I'd need to grow up quickly.

And I did.

I can hear her voice in my head. Like honey, that Southern drawl, letting me know I would need to be able to take care of myself.

I basked in her organized ways.

She calmed the chaos.

She straightened our squiggly lines and helped us make sense.

Compared with the harried, distracted, conflicted energy of my mother, trying to fit into her apron and housedress, fighting to stuff her artistic voice into the back of the closet with her working girl wardrobe, my grandma was a steady flow of calm waters. And clear direction.

I loved having her around.

Maybe those shock treatments are what broke my mom's heart. She began going in for them in her early thirties—and then developed heart disease by the time she was thirty-five. Maybe those electroshocks made her arteries constrict, decreased her blood flow, and stunted the outpouring of happy endorphins.

From then on, she took a lot of pills. At a very early age, I was aware of pill bottles by my mom's bed, always. She was forever swallowing pills. Some to help her sleep, some to thin her blood, small white nitro pills to explode open the blockages in her arteries, so she wouldn't have a heart attack. Wherever she went, they went too. She even had bejeweled cases for her pills, for when she was out and about, even just for when she traveled from room to room. They dictated her days. They shut her eyes at night. They were consistent, and consoling, prescribed to keep her engine running.

My dad, a director, was usually at work before dawn, and my mom usually slept until noon. She'd put out boxes of cereal and

Sara Lee coffee cakes the night before so we could have break-fast in the morning without waking her up. We didn't even need bowls. My brothers and I cut along the perforations on those cute little cereal boxes, poured in our milk, and chowed down right from the box.

So breakfast was peaceful.

Dinner was often another story. My mom would sit at the dinner table, pill box at her side, and pop one, two, three, four, small, white nitro pills before, during, and most definitely after a meal. Just in case, and to protect her broken heart from breaking even further, as dinnertime sometimes went way beyond sharing a meal.

It's when the scabs got ripped off. And my family let it fly.

Whatever had been brewing, festering, the air was let out of the balloon at dinnertime.

It was my mother's intention to have these family din-ners five nights a week. Usually by Wednesday, it would all go south.

"Don't upset your mother," Dad would say in a harsh whis-per. "You'll give her a heart attack."

Emotions stuffed, burden lifted, we'd scatter.

Into our own little corners, our own quiet spaces, with our dinner on TV trays, and no mention of what had gone down at the table: who got yelled at the loudest, who left the table in hys-terics, whose head fell in her plate as the family tried to act like everything was normal.

When we could manage a meal as a unit, my mom always had to sit for a time afterward to digest. She couldn't jump up from the table and clear the dishes because she might have a heart attack. (Even now I wonder: Really?)

She had a buzzer put in under the table so she could remain seated, and someone would be buzzed to clear the dishes—a housekeeper, a nanny, a daughter—whoever was around. Because of the constant threat of heart attack.

I became accustomed to living on guard. Waiting for her to go down the rabbit hole. Waiting for the shit to hit. I became adept at coping with high hysterics, managing, rearranging, orchestrating, and waiting. Always waiting. I lived with a knot in my stomach.

It still knots up.

I often have to remind myself that I can let go of it now.

From day to day, I never knew which ailment Mom was struggling with.

And on some days, there was no ailment at all.

I'd almost have a "Mom" like everyone else's Mom.

She'd be hustling and bustling, light and engaging, funny and consoling—concerned about us.

Just as I started to feel kid-like again, the change would always come.

She'd take to her bed.

The house would dim.

I couldn't have friends over because "My mom's sick."

I couldn't play too loud in the house because "My mom might have a heart attack."

The drapes were drawn.

Wanting to be close, I'd sometimes get into bed with her; my head on a pillow, on her lap, as she stroked my hair.

"My darling girl," she'd say. "I love you so."

The nighttime was a good time for her. The middle of the night. I used to love to sit with my mom in our sunken living room in front of one of the six or seven individual-size TVs we had scattered around our house. I'd wake myself up on a school night just to be with her in the quiet great room, hunched over our small set, voices low and whispery, so as not to wake the rest. She was content late at night. Neither bleary eyed nor hysterical, she was even.

Even with what her life looked like.

Even with the sometimes disappearing, sporadically rageful presence that was my dad.

Even with the passage of time and the abandonment of her dreams and passions.

Even okay with that.

She was open and thoughtful.

Interested and sage after midnight.

Gave great advice, told wicked, funny stories, held me, stroked my hair, and told me how much she loved me.

And then sometimes . . .

Complained about my dad, wondered aloud if he was faithful, told me that she wanted to die. I held her, stroked her hair, and told her how much I loved her.

When she'd fall apart, I liked it, maybe even the best.

Those times when she'd splinter. The times I could tell she

leaned on me, saying without saying, she really needed me to save her life. To give her hope.

Middle of the night was the time I felt I had her full attention.

My first music teacher, my mom was also my greatest artistic support system, and we discussed what music I should be listening to, what plays I should be reading, what movies were worth watching.

When I was in a school play or musical, she came to rehearsals and took notes.

When I wrote a new song, she listened enthusiastically and cheered me on.

She never once told me not to do what I wanted to do.

She had joy and enthusiasm for my creative pursuits, and I could intuit that my dreams were infusing her dimmed life force. Vicariously, she was breathing through me.

"You should go back to work, Mom," I'd say. "Start writing again, even if it's those dumb soap operas you used to ghostwrite. Just . . . *something*."

There was always an excuse: always another child to raise, always another reason why that wasn't a good idea—at least not just yet.

"Your father doesn't really want me to," she'd say.

But I think dissatisfaction had become her safe place.

My mom, always such a sad mystery to me. Shrouded in secrets, I never really knew what the fuck was in her head. I always felt there was more the story. Shit I just kind of made up. Something she wasn't telling me. Years later, I speculate.

But even then, as a teenager, I knew there was only so much I could do; that hers was a fragile life, and that it was only a matter of time before there would be an exit.

On the night my mother died, I went to the house in the early evening to visit or to pick up something—I can't quite remember. I'd been living in Laurel Canyon for a few years at the time. I'd moved out at seventeen and came home infrequently. I hadn't seen her in a while.

When I came into the house, she was there with my thirteen-year-old twin sisters, Liz and Jean, and they were on their way out to the movies. That seemed different to me, as did the fact that she seemed so happy. She looked beautiful and glad to see me.

"My darling girl!" she almost shrieked, wrapping me in her arms. "I've missed you."

None of that "Why haven't you called?" bullshit that other parents pulled, just pure joy at being in the same room with me. It was kind of over the top, really—not what I'd come to know of her. I figured time had passed, things with my dad had settled down, and with two of her five kids launched, she had more space for herself.

Her appearance was such a strong contrast with how she normally looked, that I took it all in.

How glowy and content she was.

How strong and healthy she looked, with color in her cheeks.

Hair washed. Makeup on.

That night would be her last.

She would never wake up again.

The next morning apparently started as usual. My little sisters waking, getting themselves breakfast, heading out the door, while Mom slept. That was nothing unusual. There was no need to knock on her door to say good-bye, no need to let her know they were leaving.

At two o'clock that afternoon, my sisters, arriving home from school, crept into my mom's bedroom on tiptoe to gently wake her and found her dead in her bed. Cause of death: heart attack in her sleep due to arteriosclerosis.

Liz told me that Mom was covered with bruises.

There was vomit sprayed across the wall above her head.

Is that what happens when you die from a heart attack in your sleep?

I'm not sure.

"Please hurry and grow up, so I can die," she used to tell my sisters.

"I can't do this anymore, I wish I was dead" had become her memorable response to any upset, real or imagined.

I'd heard it a lot in my life.

I finally just started to agree with her.

"Do it already, Mom. You are so fucking miserable."

I was fed up with all that sadness.

Suffocated by it.

She had tried to take her life, for real, twice.

That I know of.

Both times, I found her and made the calls.

Undermining my mother's wishes.

Her cries of "Leave me alone!"

"Please, don't tell your father!"

"Just let me be!"

I remember my twelve-year-old self watching as she was lifted into the ambulance.

Her eventual return home.

But I don't remember any mention of it, from anyone, to me, ever again.

When she did die, Dr. Kadish, our family doctor, and one of the people who was closest to my mom, arrived within a very short time and ruled her death a heart attack.

No talk of suicide. He loved my mom. He wouldn't have wanted to believe that. There was no autopsy. Zip the bag, shut the door, sign the paper—done.

Years later, I spoke to Dr. Kadish about my mother's death, wondering about the cause, and there was never a shift in his story. Even more years later, I tried to find my mother's medical records as a way into her history, only to be told that all records had been destroyed. They were past their expiration date.

I will never know 100 percent for sure how she met her end— and I suppose it doesn't really matter. But it does explain, for me, that final evening before her passing. It helps me understand and give resonance to the joy I felt from her, and for her.

I sometimes imagine, if she had resolved herself to an exit plan, she could have and would have allowed herself the quiet contentment of a darkened movie theater with my sisters. She would have confidently driven them all out into the night, showed up in a public place without her usual anxiety, and enjoyed herself, knowing that later in the night, she would be successful at last.

Sad no more.

I wasn't surprised my mother died so young.

I was kind of relieved.

For her.

The Director

I loved my father.

I hated my father.

I was afraid of my father.

I am just like my father.

It's complicated.

Like my dad, I am a morning person. When I was young, if I wanted to be with him, I had to wake up early to catch him before he left for work. If my mom's time with me was the deep night, my dad's was the early morning. I craved my time alone with them both and got used to sleeping odd hours so I could have them, alone, at their best. I rarely saw them at their best together.

Although he went the Hollywood way, becoming a TV director instead of accepting his overbearing mother's wish that he become a lawyer, my dad never adopted an artist's erratic habits. He was the immigrant's son; the hard worker. He'd fought for his job and the success it brought. It was not what his mother had originally intended for him but it was clearly what he wanted and was meant to be. He loved his work and was good at it. He always wanted to get out of the house in the morning and get to the set.

When it was still dark out, new again, a virginal day dawning, birds and coffee, my father would reset and see the world as possible. Enthusiastically energetic, he was bright in the morning. Fast moving, feet flying, engaged and curious, with me, about me, he saw me.

He used to make me scrambled eggs and ask me questions.

"Have you read any good books lately?" he asked me, always wanting to know what I was reading, what I was thinking.

I answered him eagerly, loving his attention.

He'd call me his special daughter, his firstborn, his oldest, his gift.

And I'd hold those moments. Like a Polaroid. *Snap!* The things he'd said. The smile he'd given me. The love he'd claimed was mine.

Even at his warmest, my dad was never an easy person. Full of contradictions. For example, his best compliment for me was "handsome." On reflection, I'm pretty sure it was a saying back then. But still, it made me feel weird. The implied masculinity of the old-school compliment stuck with me my whole life. *Why do you call me that?* I'd wonder. *Did you want a boy?*

I am his heir in so many ways, and I bloomed under the slightest nod of approval from him. The morning was the magic time when such moments of connection were possible between us.

All would be forgiven. The night before, almost forgotten.

Because by the evening, he was gone, my morning dad.

The man who came home after work was a bleary, snarling, exhausted, and intolerant slammer of doors. When his arrival was imminent, I hid out in my room, listening intently, cocooned in the safe womb of the dark purple bedspread and drapes I had chosen. Mercurial and hair triggered, he had to be read closely. Never quite sure what set off what, I stood guard. Behind doors, under beds, waiting to hear his footsteps through the door, I became adept at reading steps. By the weight of his gait, I could tell if I'd be criticized or praised. Safe to enter his space or best to slip out the back.

When I read it wrong, happened into the crosshairs of his anger accidentally, I froze, waiting for the barrage of disparaging comments that sometimes came.

"You're too much," he said to me, my siblings, my mother, exhausted after long hours of what he declared, "doing what I love."

"It's all your fault," he said.

"I have to work so hard," he sighed.

The five of us and my mother, just all . . . "too much."

We all took our turns pushing back when he lost his shit. Very rarely was there a compromising response from him.

Ultimately, he was "the papa."

We backed down in the name of "respect for your elders." His constant reminder.

We never said anything to defend ourselves. Just took it all in when he yelled. Nobody outside our family knew how loud it got at my house. Though I'm sure it was loud at a lot of houses on the block. That was how it was then. Everybody was screaming, and nobody was talking about it.

Those were the days.

Dad loved his job, but it was high pressure, which took its toll on him, and on all of us. As did his fear that his success would vanish. Or that whatever current job he had would be his last.

He cradled that burden.

He was imprinted with a superstitious way of thinking that came along with Eastern European Jewish tradition, which cast a shadow on everything he accomplished.

The *kina hora*.

The evil eye.

I believe that my father was born with a grounding in the Jewish faith, but as with so many Jewish families who suffered atrocities in Eastern Europe, his family had lost their faith along the way. With nothing to protect them spiritually, having abandoned a belief in God, as they believed they'd been abandoned, they turned to rituals and superstitions.

That went kind of like this:

Don't say something positive, or you will tempt fate.

The evil eye will make your worst fears come true.

Don't speak too loudly about your success. If you let people know you're doing well, it might just be taken away.

Don't be greedy and ask for too much.

Don't be a braggart.

Humility, bordering on humiliation, for accomplishments achieved.

Considering the ramifications of this kind of thinking—
passed on to me and ingrained in me—makes a lot of things make
sense.

My perceptions.

Why celebrity has never been my comfortable place.

Why being able to accept a compliment has been a learned
behavior.

Why I don't want anyone to know how much love I need.

Why, for many years, I tried to quiet myself down, as I'd
been told to do.

Even though it was nearly impossible.

Some people are at their best at home. Not my dad. Large and
in charge, he really was at his best at work. I didn't understand
what my father did until I was old enough to visit and sit still on
the set and not talk when the red light was on (the really hard
part at that age). Seeing Dad on the set, I kind of fell in love
with him from that point on. He was so engaging and revered
at work. And everybody wanted to make him happy, just like I
did at home.

My dad directed some of the great early television shows,
starting with *Playhouse 90*, *The Twilight Zone*, and *Peter Gunn*.
I loved to visit when he was directing *Dr. Kildare* or *The Man
from Uncle*. In fact, Richard Chamberlain was my social ace in the
hole with some of the unapproachable cool girls in my elementary school. I bribed friendships out of them with visits to meet
Dr. Kildare himself.

I was a shy kid. I always felt invisible, and in social situations, my timid nature easily came undone. But in the presence of my daddy's TV star friends, I was considered. And considered was a step forward. I got prettier, chattier, way more desirable to those little bitches who never wanted to be my friend at school for my merits alone. It was no wonder I, like my dad, loved his hard-earned job.

The world was a scary place for a little Russian boy who came to America at the age of seven displaced, unfamiliar. His name had been Boris, but when they got to America, his mom changed his name to Bernard. To fit in. To be a part of. Must be weird to feel hidden at that age. Could make you feel ashamed of who you are. I imagine that might have been a struggle. Losing a sense of who you are and all you are familiar with at such a young age could cut deep—along with my very strong, opinionated Yiddish grandmother imposing her sense of right and wrong, what worked, what didn't, what it meant to "be an American." What they had to do as a family to be seen as appropriate in this new world they now called home. Obstinate and strict, Grandma Rose pushed my father hard. In the name of moving him toward excellence, she busted his balls and left him never feeling up to snuff.

When my dad's family escaped from the Soviet Union, he didn't speak English. No one in his family did. Rose spoke only Yiddish and very broken English throughout her life, and he was the only person in his family to ever really learn English.

They'd been through a lot, my dad and my grandparents. I imagine that the family fled Russia in response to the repressive regime of dictator Joseph Stalin. (Once again, I have no one to ask, so it's all speculation.) They brought very little with them. The one thing I remember they had from home was the big samovar: the large silver tea maker that it seemed like every Russian family owned. They left behind my dad's three brothers, all of military age. Two were killed in World War II. My uncle Daniil, who entertained the troops, went on to become a movie star in Russia.

They landed in Detroit. My dad's dad, Rose's husband, Lewis, came first, and once he had a job and a place to live, he sent for Rose and his youngest son. In Russia, Lewis had been a cantor and a sometime painter and contractor. In America, he worked as a house painter. Rose had been a ballet dancer in Russia, but in her new country, she became a union rep for the United Automobile Workers, helping to organize and support the factory employees. They worked very hard and had very little money. Living hand to mouth, life was tough, but it was better than where they'd come from, and in that, there was joy.

There was gratitude.

There was freedom.

And real appreciation for every penny earned.

But, too, worry and woe over every dollar spent. Financial security being the ultimate fulfillment—food on the table, a roof over their heads—far outweighed the satisfaction to be attained from work you loved. As my godfather, Norman Lear, points out, the mandate of the Yiddish immigrant was to be "a good provider."

In Detroit, they became involved with the Yiddish cultural movement, which emphasized Jewish heritage and the Yiddish language. As a child, Dad studied Yiddish language, drama, and culture.

In the early 1940s, Lewis was diagnosed with emphysema and told by his doctors that he needed a warmer climate to survive. They left Detroit and moved to the Los Angeles neighborhood of Boyle Heights, which is now a Hispanic area, but in the forties and fifties, it was completely Jewish. Eventually they ended up in Venice, California.

In my dad's family, it was all about security and making money. Education increased your financial opportunities. So my dad was on a scholarly path, as his mother insisted. Rose wanted her very bright, hardworking son to become a doctor or a lawyer, something substantial and seriously American dreamish. Education being the Holy Grail, he dutifully followed the straight line laid out in front of him—until he couldn't do it anymore. He spent years sticking to his mother's plan before finally setting out on his own path. Not unlike what his rebellious daughter would do years later.

In his heart, an artistic yearning grew, maybe inherited from Lewis the cantor, Rose the dancer, and his brother the actor, a stirring desire for a theatrical pursuit. To be in the arts. Perhaps all those years of hiding as "Bernard" were actually appealing. The idea of playing pretend might have felt familiar, as it would for me when I found my own calling as an actor. Maybe he was responding to the draw of poetry and romance through the plays he loved to read. Or maybe, just simply, it was that my dad loved women. And the theater was where the girls were.

For whatever reason, he was bit by the bug.

He followed his growing passions on the sly. In the shadows, hidden from the watchful wishes of his mother, he found theater classes and theater folks to hang with while at UCLA. I don't know exactly when, but at some point, he also took back his real name, Boris.

My father continued his studies and somehow got himself into Harvard Law School. Dad had not even wanted to apply, but his mother made him. He had okay grades, not great. But one of his history professors at UCLA, who was a big deal, thought Dad was brilliant and wrote him a recommendation that got him in on a scholarship. Otherwise, Harvard would have been impossible to afford.

While he was studying law, he had several jobs, including working for a small newspaper and at a shoe store, but it was never enough. My father was so poor that when he wanted to take a girl on a date, he had to find a friend with money to go with them and then charm the friend into paying for the whole date. (My dad was a charmer, a trait he benefitted from his entire life.)

Midway through law school, Dad abruptly took a turn, dropped out, and was accepted to the Yale School of Drama, all unbeknownst to his mother.

Wide swings my old man made.

A stronger sense of self bubbling up.

An undeniable itch.

He eventually went toe-to-toe with Rose and stayed on his path—not hers. Dad was happier, and he didn't care that financial advancement seemed a bigger risk in this new world he had found. He forged ahead.

After all that schooling, my father drove a cab during the day and directed Yiddish theater by night. During this time, he met my mom. She was working for Norman Lear, the writer and producer who went on to create TV hits including *All in the Family* and *The Jeffersons*, and *The Martin and Lewis Show*. Norman introduced them, having met my father through his connection with the Yiddish theater. My mom and dad were really in love. And she helped to complete the vision that Dad saw of himself, living a creative life.

I don't think my dad ever doubted his chosen path. But quickly, the reality of life as an artist with a new wife, which was followed shortly by a baby, sometimes made him question whether an academic path might not have brought him a broader sense of security. I think these questions were what later made him worry about me and my future security.

Grandma Rose hadn't seen "movie and TV director" coming, and she could never understand it. His love and desire to be in the theater blindsided her. She barely acknowledged it. She never really saw him.

Never would.

Never understood him.

Ego makes it hard for us to just let our children be who they are. That was especially true for my grandparents' generation, which had such high expectations. I'm careful not to put that kind of pressure on my own kids, but things were different back then. Even at the height of his success, when we were living in our cush house on the Westside of LA, Grandma Rose would rag on Dad about having dropped out of Harvard Law to study to be an actor at the Yale Drama School. Might as well have been going to clown school. Better to be a circus performer. Same thing, really, in her eyes.

Until the day she died, she haunted my dad with the same question: "What do you do?" she'd inflect in her broken, Yiddishy English.

"Director, is that a real job?" she'd whine.

"What kind of job *eees* that?"

"Director of what?"

Rose never forgave him for deviating from the path she'd wished for him. Could never meet him where he wanted to go in his life. Their move to America had cut them off from all formal ties to his Jewishness, as Rose became a union-organizing Socialist, but he would occasionally search for something to believe in. Some higher form of worship than his job. And for his children to be exposed to. We'd occasionally drop into a temple. We'd have a Shabbat dinner at a friend's house. But never Hanukah, never Hebrew school, nothing consistent. When I was about thirteen, Dad decided he wanted to try sharing a Passover Seder with us kids. He bought a recording of Passover services conducted by a rabbi named Moishe Oishe. We were to follow along to the service on the record. My grandmother was invited, and I watched as she belittled and made fun of my dad. Called him names and laughed in his face for having a curious mind about the faith she had long ago abandoned.

It was terrible.

He was diminished in front of his children.

It was the first time I empathized with my dad, and years later, it allowed me to finally understand why his parenting style frequently diminished us. He was doing what had been done to him. He knew no better.

Parenting has no guidebook; we come to it with what came at us.

It's only the conscious mind that can shift the paradigm.

As a parent, I understand the concept of guidance. As very small children, we are the opinions, habits, routines of our parents. But also, as very small children, I believe younger than acknowledged, we start to find our own mojo, our own path, and I tried to acknowledge that in my own kids. See them for who they are instead of who I wanted to see. My dad was more of a "my way or the highway" kind of dad. While he knew the way he was raised was limited, he was never able to fully transcend his upbringing when it came to raising his own kids.

I was able to do it differently. And I did.

Who were my dad and I to each other? I have stories about him, family lore, but there are only a few actual shared experiences I can recall. The really memorable moments I had with him were when he met me where I was, in my world: music. The first was when he introduced me to Ella Fitzgerald at the age of nine or ten by giving me an album, *Ella Fitzgerald Sings Cole Porter*. It might have been my first record, even before *Meet the Beatles*. I played it endlessly, and he'd listen to it with me. He'd dance with me, too, up in my room, singing along: "Birds do it, bees do it, even educated fleas do it."

I loved that dad.

He also took me on a "daddy date" when I was twelve. We went to the famous music club the Troubadour in West Hollywood to hear Nina Simone. I was thrilled. It was new and exciting to be out with just my dad. And to have it be something that I was really interested in and passionate about, music, made me feel seen and understood by him in a way I was not used to.

Good or bad, what always mattered was to feel my dad's eyes on me. I can still remember how it felt to be seen by him, although it didn't happen as often as I wanted. But I can't remember the feeling of seeing *him*, or exactly what he looked like. I can look at a photograph and be reminded. He was medium—not tall, not short. He was handsome—not drop-dead perfect gorgeous, not Marlboro Man, but handsome. Women liked him. Always the charmer, remember.

Unlike the way I can easily recall my mother's small hands on mine, or her sad brown eyes that always looked half shut, I can't pull up the same specifics about my dad. I think it's weird that I can't see him. It makes me sad and very aware of just how long it's been since he passed: 1981.

More than thirty years.

That's a long time. And memories do fade.

But it also makes me wonder if I ever really knew him.

Just like I'm convinced he never understood who I was or who I was striving to become.

I loved my father; I was just never really sure that he loved me.

I think he loved the me he thought I could be; the me that wasn't actually me.

He loved me when I did things his way. But from a young age, that was never my way. Born rebellious from the jump, I always had a different idea. Just like he'd had from the way Grandma Rose lived.

I am he. But I think, by the time he was my dad, he'd forgotten that about himself. He'd forgotten that he was the guy who'd always had a different idea, too.

When I was a teenager and found myself called to be a musician, my father did as his mother had done with him and tried to change my path. My dad, an artist himself, thought it was crazy to pursue a career in music.

He didn't have much faith in my dreams of rock stardom, and he wasn't sure if health insurance would be included, but he knew that it would be important. My dad, the successful TV and film director, decided that if he could help me get an acting gig and a union card, I could get health insurance. It was his way of helping his "artistic" daughter in a practical way. So when I was seventeen, he cast me in a TV movie called *The Failing of Raymond*, starring Jane Wyman and Dean Stockwell, playing a girl in a mental institution, bleary eyed and comatose, with maybe a line or two.

"So you can get a union card," he said.

This meant I had health insurance. But I only remember feeling shame that I'd gotten a job so many yearned for because of my dad. I wasn't proud of myself for doing that movie (even though, checking it out on YouTube, I was pretty good). I was embarrassed. I also did an episode of *Columbo*, the crime show starring Peter Falk.

Nepotism served me well, and I got my Screen Actors Guild card and health insurance.

Dad thought I had some talent, having seen me in a few leading roles in my high school productions, mostly all musicals. In hindsight, I realize that all his cajoling and insisting, which I interpreted as pushy and undermining, were just his way of helping his strong-willed "special firstborn." He did the best that he could, as he saw it.

I think I had some acting talent, too. But I didn't really take the skill seriously at that time.

Because, by now, I was in a band.

And by that age, the fact that acting brought me closer to my dad wasn't much of a draw. I was all about putting distance between myself and my family, all about getting free, and the best way I knew how to do that was through music.

What I really wanted was for him to acknowledge me as a musician, and he could never do that. Maybe, he was judging himself—and me—by his own mother's words, because they really got to him in the end. Because he now knew how hard the artist's path was, he was worried for me. Looking back now, I wonder if maybe my father recognized more of himself in me than I realized at that age. Wanted me to choose the actor's life, rather than music, because then he could at least give me a hand up.

Other than the six months of drama school my dad strong-armed me into, I never stopped pursuing my heart's desire, music.

And that path took me away from home. He was disapproving, so I didn't let him get near my tender dreams.

My mom died when I was twenty-one. Although my dad remarried within the first year and a half after she passed, it actually took him years to recover. He moved, and suddenly the family house was gone. By the time I was twenty-two, I had met my first husband, Freddie, and I had married him by twenty-three. My dad threw me the wedding. But most of the time, we were very disconnected. We dealt with our grief not by coming together but by attaching ourselves to other people.

When I was in my midtwenties, out of nowhere, my father started to call me on the phone, just to talk: "Hey, sweetheart. Just wanted to call and see how you were."

Startled, I almost didn't know how to answer. *Like, really, how am I?* Then, as the conversation continued, the tone would deepen, prompted by him.

"No, how are you really?" he asked once, a question I couldn't remember my father ever having asked me so sincerely before.

As we began to dialogue more and more, as his phone calls became more frequent, I heard that my detached pop was seeking spirituality. He was vulnerable and curious. For the first time, he was questioning his belief in the black hole he had thought the journey ended in. He was reconsidering. He was wondering if maybe, just maybe, there might be more.

And finally, I was old enough to just listen, without the over-burdening need to be seen and understood. As I'd always done, as I'd never thought he did—see me—understand me. I was finally able to know he did.

See me.

I could feel he loved me.

And I loved him.

His spiritual seeking touched the seeker within me. He was talking to me about God. He had just started therapy. These were things I had reached for, that my dad had never believed in. While my mother was constantly in therapy and in pursuit of something to make her feel safe and comfortable, sometimes bumping up against her higher self, he had never understood and even pooh-poohed it. So the fact that he was looking deeper now gave me compassion and made me bond with him.

Just as I was finally getting to know the guy—just as I was finally not afraid of him, as his softer, sweeter, older side started to emerge—the phone rang one day in May 1981.

My brother Joey and I were roommates at the time (my marriage to Freddie having expired), and we were both at home. Dad was in Bend, Oregon, shooting on location for the TV movie *World War III*, so the call must have been from someone in the film's production office.

"Your dad's been in an accident, but we think he's okay," the person said.

We were upset and scared, but we figured it would be okay, like the voice on the phone had said.

But ten minutes later, the phone rang again.

"It's more serious than we thought," the person said. "You kids should come here. We're sending a car for you."

Joey and I were picked up and driven to the airport. We called one more time before getting on the plane to check the status. We got news that things were getting worse, but no one would tell us what had happened. When we landed in Oregon a few hours later, somebody picked us up and drove us to the hospital.

He had just died. He was fifty-seven.

It was only then that we learned Dad had jumped out of a helicopter prematurely, before the blades had stopped completely. And because he was on top of a mountain where the air was thin, and he was disoriented, when he turned back to get his script, left on the seat of the helicopter, he walked the wrong way right into the spinning blade. He went unconscious immediately. The whole thing was surreal.

Just like that, he was gone, just as he and I were starting to get to know each other.

Today, though, more than three decades later, I have started to realize and feel the ways in which he is always with me.

I see his Cheshire cat grin.

I hear his critical words.

I feel the illumination and warmth of being in his orbit when he shined his attention on me.

I feel the painful distance when he took that attention away from me.

He was tough. Hard to please, tough on me. Tough on himself.

He could never live up to his mom's expectations. I never felt I could live up to his. But my dad pushed back. And, in hindsight, he taught me how to do the same.

See, I do see him, even if he didn't live to share that feeling of being seen with me.

And maybe he saw more of me than I ever realized.

I have become him in so many ways.

Truly, daddy's girl.

Not just the me he was trying to shape or the me that I was getting to; the me that I always was.

Maybe he saw more of me than I ever realized.

My Saving Grace

One afternoon at my Girl Scout meeting when I was ten or eleven, I arrived with my guitar, just as I always had. In the hallway, I took it out and left the case outside the door. I entered the school community room with the guitar slung over my shoulder, next to my badge sash. I had minimal badges, maybe "Cooking" and "Painting."

At a previous meeting, I had sung to the girls during the "getting to know you" part, to much appreciation. I assumed they would want to hear more, like at every meeting. That would be my spot. Singer. Just like the other girls were good at sewing, first aid, citizenship, social skills. My skill was music.

Midmeeting, after all the formalities, it was time for sharing.

Sharing—the talking kind—was the last thing I felt able to do. I held my guitar close, like a friend, its warm wood and curved body reassuring me I wasn't alone. I strummed my wooden friend, took a deep breath, and launched into the latest tune my mom had passed down to me, "Long Black Veil."

She walks these hills, in a long black veil
Visits my grave when the night winds wail . . .

"*Stop!*" the den mother said.

The room fell silent.

"This is not the time *or* place for that kind of sharing, entertaining," she said. "Please put the guitar away."

My eyes filled with tears as I sheepishly walked out the door. I felt kicked in the stomach and needed a minute. In that moment, not even my guitar could protect me, and it would be years before I learned how to say "Fuck you." I knew I was supposed to put my guitar back in its case. Instead, I did what I always did when I wanted to feel better. I sat down on the linoleum floor in the hallway and strummed to myself. I found myself singing another song my mom had recently taught me. I almost sang out full voice, mimicking the way my mom had delivered the song, a folky blues with a slight yodel.

Down in the valley, the valley so low,
Hang your head over, hear the wind blow.
Hear the wind blow, dear, hear the wind blow,
Hang your head over, hear the wind blow.
Roses love sunshine, violets love dew,
Angels in heaven, know I love you.

Just like that, my guitar's magic powers were returned to me. It didn't matter that my mom wasn't with me or if I had an audience or not. There was a special relationship between the music and me that made everything hard a little easier, everything scary a little safer. I sang and I sang, calming myself. And I never went back into that room.

I decided at a very young age, *This is who I am: a musician.* After learning to play the guitar from my mom when I was ten, I brought it with me everywhere: school show-and-tell, my brief foray into the Girl Scouts. Anywhere I might be required to talk to anyone, I'd bring my guitar. Talking made me nervous, but I loved to sing and play.

When I was thirteen, I taught myself to play the piano. I loved to play all the minor keys—the black ones—because everything sounded good on them. They had a sorrowful dissonance that matched my moody heart and were easy to make sense of. I didn't know what I was doing, but I could make it sound like I did. I started writing songs. Coincidentally, this was also around the time my parents decided I was fat and needed diet pills. I remained pudgy, but prolific, fueled by cigarettes and the amphetamines. By the age of fourteen, I was writing a song a day.

I read *The Book* by Alan Watts, and Hermann Hesse's *Narcissus and Goldmund,* and was constantly writing in journals about how I was looking for deeper meaning. I wanted to be Laura Nyro or Joni Mitchell. Laura Nyro, mostly, because of her urban, blue-eyed soul sound that reminded me of my first influences, Ella Fitzgerald and Nina Simone. She wailed, almost like she was crying. I wore all black, like her—and like all of the other pudgy Jewish girls who loved her for making them feel like she was expressing just for them.

I banged away on my piano so much that my parents moved it into my room. It felt like a supportive move on their part. Most likely, they just needed a door to shut on all my teen angst. In my purple bedroom, with matching curtains and bedspread, my brown upright and me, I left all else behind. I smoked Marlboro Reds, hidden from sight, smoke blown out the window through a little crack. All I wrote about was boys. It's embarrassing. I sang the stories of made-up love affairs. These were songs of unrequited love, going from falling madly in love to breaking up in the space of just one verse and chorus.

In high school, especially, music became my personality. I felt hollow and aimless without it, awkward and antisocial. I'd sit on the lawn during lunch and play my guitar and sing rather than socialize. I'd drive my old Chevy Nova to the end of the city, sit on the beach until the sun went down, and sing and strum the same songs over and over, like "Pleasant Street," an early tune by singer-songwriter Tim Buckley. Or a Crosby, Stills & Nash song, with my buddy Johnny Segal, who years later, through the most bizarre circumstance, became a sponsor of mine in recovery.

By the time I was fifteen, I was in a band. To this day, I don't know how they found me, but I'm so grateful they did. The guys in the group had already graduated from high school. Still a high school student myself. With my guitar in my hand, I felt confident and right among these older guys. My voice, and my passion for the music they loved too, were my keys to earning my place with them: the bassist, Bob; the guitarist Frank; and the singer-guitarist, Patrick.

I loved all the guys in the band, but I loved Bob the bass player the most. One Saturday afternoon, I think it was at Frank's house, big, tall, handsome Bob stood close to me. I could feel his breath, feel his backbeat, and his flirtation. We sang on the microphone together, our mouths close, our voices entwined, my knees shaking. As I write this, I feel gooseflesh rising on my arms. It comes back to me, whole.

Music was my key to everything. For me, it was like connecting the dots: an introduction to sexuality. My voice, my heart, my sex—a perfect trine.

My passions: music and guys.

My friend Rick Fleishman introduced me to the songs of Robert Johnson and stirred in me a deep love for blues music. I'd go to Rick's house after school, and he'd play me blues records and show me blues guitar chords. There was something in the blues for me that I could finally name: I had the blues.

And Rick didn't try to tell me that the blues didn't belong to me. My Depression-era parents had the attitude that I had nothing to complain about because I had a roof over my head and enough food to eat. What they couldn't understand was the blues went deeper than that, and the blues belonged to everyone who needed it.

Soon I was escaping to a folk, blues, and rock club in Hollywood called the Ash Grove (now the world-famous Improv comedy club). Blues clubs were cool clubs, and so I felt cool just for being there. I'd catch J. B. Hutto and His Hawks, Taj Mahal, and Willie Dixon, a round, happy dude who played a stand-up bass and was like a big teddy bear.

I went to the club frequently with my best friend, Rasma, the hippest chick I knew in high school and my partner in blues love. She was a year older than me, sixteen, and could drive. We'd show up, two white girls from Pacific Palisades High. But we felt like we were right where we belonged. Our love for the music gave us entrance.

Definitely underage, and not at all shy around my newfound heroes, I can remember slammin' back a few swigs with these guys out of somebody's brown paper bag of wine in the alleyway behind the club. One night in that alleyway, Willie Dixon and his harmonica player, Big Walter "Shaky" Horton, stumbled upon us, two young girls, smokin' our Marlboro Reds, trying to get some air after the Chicago Blues All-Stars blew us away.

"Hello, ladies," said Walter. "Enjoying the show?"

Startled, a little high on reefer, and sweaty, trying to be cool, we answered "Hmmm-huh."

Big Walter took a swig from that bottle in the paper bag and offered it our way. It was dark, and we must have looked older than we were.

Willie, Cheshire cat grinnin'. "Want some?" said Walter.

The floodgates opened. Raz fawned: "Man, you guys killed it! We are such big fans. 'Hoochie Coochie Man,' 'I Can't Quit You Baby,' 'Wang Dang Doodle.'"

"You girls like the blues?" asked Big Walter. "Ain't you girls a little far from home?"

"Oh no," said Raz. "She sings the blues." Pointed at me.

I died a little. And took a big swig out of that bag.

Willie laughed. Walter encouraged me to "Hum somethin'."

"Oh no, not in front of you guys. I mean, you are, ya know, you guys," I said and died a little more.

For the first time, Willie spoke, kind of grandfatherly, protective, all knowing: "You'll get there, girl. Just keep doin' what you love."

"I love the sad songs," I said.

"Everybody gets the blues sometimes," he said. "It's good to let folks know."

And just like that, I was gobsmacked.

Always respectful and definitely amused by my fifteen-year-old adoration, these dudes looked out for me. But they didn't treat me like a kid, so I didn't really know they were looking out for me. I felt connected and accepted by them. Rasma and I found camaraderie in that bluesy community that drew us in and made us feel right at home.

Years later, I would become very good friends with Susan and Clifford Antone, owners of Antone's, the beloved blues club in

Austin, Texas. They introduced me to all the greats. I had dinner at their house with Muddy Waters. He was quiet and gentlemanly and so grateful to be embraced by the Antones' love of blues. There was always a stage for him to play there.

I got on the tour bus with grumpy Albert King. Partied a bit too hard with Bobby "Blue" Bland. Had a short but sweet love affair with guitarist Jimmie Vaughan, which I'm sure neither of us can barely remember. After all, it was the early eighties.

I love and am uplifted by blues music. Always will be.

I straddled the music and drama departments in high school, and I was in school productions. But I never thought it was cool. I was embarrassed by the "drama kids." They all seemed too shiny. Being in that band my junior year of high school with handsome Bob, the bass player, now, *that* was where I found my cool.

I wasn't the lead singer. But I was part of the band. I'd sing some solos, lots of harmonies, tambourines, maracas—shake, shake, shake. I loved being in a band. Still do.

It felt/feels familial, organized, communal, loving, bonding—all the things I longed for from my family.

I had never fit in with a clique.

I had never played on a sports team.

But being in a band, playing music with other people makes me feel connected to the earth.

So when it was time to think about college, I didn't. I just kept

writing songs and hoping that soon I'd have my own band . . .
somehow. When I was seventeen, I graduated from high school.
That summer, I moved out of my parents' house.

My father had convinced me to look at a school called
Cal Arts in Valencia, California. And when I say convinced, I
mean threatened to cut me off financially if I didn't. A school of
conservatory-type programs in theater, dance, music, and visual
arts, you didn't need high SAT scores or an outstanding GPA to
get in. You got in by auditioning. I thought it might be cool to
be in the music school. My father said he would only allow me
(pay for me) to go if I went into the theater program. He clearly
saw something in me from all my high school productions that I
didn't see. I figured if I got in, I'd sneak my way into the music
school and bootleg classes. I also thought I'd never get in in the
first place.

I approached that college audition with no attachments. I had
no real desire to study acting. No fear of rejection. My attitude
was light and breezy, unencumbered by expectation. Loosey-
goosey. I can't remember what my audition was, but it might have
been the dark Elizabeth Proctor that I'd played in *The Crucible* in
high school. Or Lady Macbeth, for which I'd won a high school
Shakespeare award. Either way, I didn't put a lot of effort into it,
just recited a monologue I already knew. (Years later, when I was
approached to audition for my first serious acting job on a TV
show, *Mary*, starring Mary Tyler Moore, I had the same attitude.
Actually more like, "Are you kidding? I'm not even looking for
a job as an actor. I'm a musician!" Apparently that approach is
gold for me.)

So at age eighteen, I got into the theater department at Cal Arts. I loved parts of it.

Paul Reubens and David Hasselhoff were both in my acting class. Paul was my fantastically colorful best buddy down the hall from me in the dorm. And David was a very sweet guy from the Midwest who was very enthusiastic!

We had an amazing mentor-teacher named Beatrice Manley, and we weaved our way through sense memory, scene study, movement classes—even fencing—for crazy long hours every day. It was intense.

But conservatory was conservatory. They wouldn't actually let me audit music classes. So, at night, I'd have to make my escape, as much as possible, to the rooms where pianos were tucked away.

I had a roommate, a cello player, who had boyfriends. Plural. They used to have sex in the room when I was there. So I used to jump up in search of an escape. Paul would go with me. We'd smoke pot and find a piano, and I'd bang away on the keys, writing my forlorn, bluesy songs of woe. Paul used to love to sit on the bench beside me and have me sing my songs for him. He was my big fan. Paul's love and friendship for me was a bridge.

School was all too much for me. Learning the craft of acting involves a lot of things, a process of self-discovery being the biggest requirement: looking deep into your own personal emotional life in order to mine the feelings, and bringing them to bear on the lives of those lurking in the imagination of the playwright or screenwriter. It's courageous to go deep. I was too young, too veiled, too self-protected, to stand in the middle of myself.

In one sense-memory class, the carpeted classroom was darkened, the shades drawn, and we were to imagine ourselves back inside the womb. (Of course, my mother's womb had been smoke filled, as with almost all women of her time. So, just like the womb, but sans smoke.)

While the twelve of us were lying on the floor in the fetal position, the teacher verbally guided us all to imagine the warm, cozy, safe feeling of being tucked in tight to our own little wombs. Once safely ensconced, we were to imagine pushing our way out and through. We wormed and wiggled on the floor. We didn't make noise. We were being reborn.

The point of the exercise was to sharpen our senses; to experience everything for the first time. But I ended up in a fetal position, crying hysterically and frozen because I didn't want to come out of my womby safe place. I had to be talked down from the exercise. Class had ended, lights came back on, and I was still in a corner in a ball. The world wasn't the same as that smoke-filled womb. Maybe my lovely mother wasn't fully equipped to hold her first baby. And this is what the exercise invoked: those early years, real or imagined. Whatever it had brought up, I didn't like it, and I wanted to stuff it back inside.

Growing up, I had found a way to survive the empty spaces in my family and in myself, to not look too closely at my external or internal circumstances. Acting school started to blow my cover. Open my eyes. Shine a light where I was afraid to go.

I lasted one semester.

I dropped out and went to work.

I got a gig as a chorus girl and understudy in the Broadway touring company of the rock musical *Two Gentlemen of Verona*, based on the Shakespeare play, with music by Galt MacDermot, who'd written the music for *Hair*. I blinked and was in a theater in New York, rehearsing. When I try to recall the experience, I have a sense of complete terror, masked by ballsy bravado fueled by my continued use of diet pills and cigarettes.

It was a *rock* musical. So in my mind, I was closer to my dream of rock star status than fucking theater school, but it was a stretch. I was still in the theater, which I wasn't fully down with. Musical theater peeps really weren't cool. I proudly wore my rock-chick attitude, black clothes and cigs, and just really did my best to not be a part of it.

We actually do end up where we're supposed to be in this life. At least I have. Being an actor has clearly been my path, and I so desperately didn't want it to be. Foolish little girl.

Thank God for amphetamines and alcohol at that time in my life. They both gave me courage. In recovery, there is a term: "Act as if." It's a tool for getting through shit that feels unbearable. When I heard it, it seemed natural to me. That had been my whole life: "Acting as if" I knew what the fuck I was doing in the world. What the fuck to do onstage in a Broadway show. Even the little things. Socializing. Things that required connection. Intimate things. Making friends. What to wear. What to eat. Who to be. Even now, I'm "acting as if" I know how to write a book.

When I got the part in *Two Gents*, not only had I been hired to sing and dance from the top tier of the scaffolding that was the set (and I am deathly afraid of heights), but also I was the understudy for one of the leads, which required me to show up for every rehearsal and learn her every move, just in case! I was both enamored and overburdened by the responsibility. I kept wondering, *Isn't she ever going to get sick? I hope she gets sick. Oh fuck, what if she gets sick?*

But she never got sick.

Typical for being on the road, once the show had opened, daytime was free time. We never needed to be at the theater until six o'clock for an eight o'clock curtain. About eight months into our nine-month run , we were in San Francisco on a Friday afternoon. I was staying in the apartment of friends of friends from Cal Arts for our two-week stay in SF. So I'm hangin' out with a few new SF buddies, smokin' weed, early enough in the day to be bright eyed by six, when I was due at the theater. And the telephone rang.

"Well, tonight's your night, girl. Finally, after all these months, she's sick!" the stage manager said with more excitement than I could tolerate.

"Really?" I moaned, feigning identical enthusiasm. "How great."

In my altered weed state, I'm sure I laughed for a minute and then broke out in a sweat.

After months of my complaining, "This bitch will never go down," she had.

I didn't feel as sure-footed as I had imagined I would be, and the pot didn't help.

But by the time I got onstage, I had sobered up, straight as an arrow. And I felt at home, hitting my marks, knowing my lines, feeling confident, as I always did when I would actually get onstage, amid the make believe of it all. Second nature, as it had always been.

During the countrywide nine-month run with that show, my roommate was another soon-to-be TV star, Joanna Kerns. Blonde, blue eyed, and cheerful, she and I couldn't have been more like night and day. But I liked her. I felt safe being around someone so wholesome.

She grounded me. Helped me to peel back some of that cool exterior I wore so defiantly.

Joanna came from a sports background, with all the discipline and structure that entails. As much as they were foreign to me, I had a craving for those regimes and preparations. I watched, and learned, out of the corner of my eye.

Because God forbid somebody thinks I don't know it all. There I am, constantly "acting as if."

There is no better training for performance than being in a live onstage theatrical production. No television show or movie set I've ever been on has required the same amount of focus and commitment that the theater demands. There is no second take on opening night. There is no "Don't worry, they'll fix it in the mix."

I complained about it, but I really liked it.

I liked the focus of the moment, terrifying as it was.

The fact that *Two Gentlemen of Verona* was a Tony Award–winning theatrical production somewhat satisfied my dad.

The gig at least helped to upgrade me to second-class citizen in his eyes. A step up from college dropout. I proudly presented my first paycheck to him, hoping to receive a small "Attaboy." But he just couldn't help himself. His response was the usual: "Well, that's great, but then what are you going to do?" I could never really satisfy him. Him, who I have spent my whole life trying to please.

The moment, never fully appreciated.

I suppose my father's attitude did teach me the benefits of "having a plan" and kept me driving forward. But it also gave me the sense that nothing was ever good enough. It's taken me years to want and appreciate what I have. Right here, right now. Instead of always thinking that the next thing will be better.

After the touring production ended, in the fall of my twentieth year, I got a job as a singing waitress. There was a restaurant in Santa Monica called the Great American Food and Beverage Co. All the staff had special talents. Magicians, comics, songwriters, poets. The deal was that you would serve the food, or wipe down the table, or bus the dishes, or sling the hash, and then stop everything and perform. You had to audition to get a job there. And no restaurant experience was required. Lucky for me—because I had none.

I turned out to be a for-shit waitress.

Intolerant and clumsy.

But I could sing.

My saving grace was my talent. Once again, as through most of my life, my skill as a performer found me friends and, always, forgiveness. My talent has always gotten me off the hook. I could get your order wrong, spill blue cheese dressing on your lap, whisper under my breath "what an asshole" you were, and then pick up my guitar or go to the piano and sing you an awesome rendition of Van Morrison's "Brown Eyed Girl." You'd tip me big and forget all about my sloppy, rude behavior. It was like the rest of my life. How I got by.

So I was a singing waitress. Alongside Danny Elfman, who became a dynamo of a composer (he and the other members of his band Oingo Boingo all worked there); Rickie Lee Jones; Matthew Wilder, who went on to produce No Doubt; and many more supertalented folks would rotate through on their way to anywhere else. At least at the Great American, you could still call yourself an artist while waiting tables.

One night in 1975, Gene Simmons from the new band Kiss came to the restaurant after playing a gig as the opening act at the Santa Monica Civic Auditorium. It was their second tour.

I was their waitress, and Gene decided I was to be his.

When you heard me sing, you'd generally like me. Sometimes want to date me. That was my calling card. Maybe my weight wasn't as perfect as my dad wanted it to be, or I wasn't as "book smart" as my Harvard-educated brother, David, whom Dad admired openly. But I could get your attention with my voice. I loved to sing. I knew I was talented. I wanted to feel better about myself, and although I couldn't always silence my own critical voices, when I sang, they were overtaken.

When Gene saw me in the restaurant that night, before I had sung for him, he was flirting, I could tell. After I'd sung for him, he saw my talent. Then I had two things he liked. A kind of sassy, badass, cute chick and a voice. I took him home with me that night because he was quite persuasive.

At first, I thought Gene was really weird. Nobody knew who Kiss was back then. They just wore a lot of makeup. But he was cute and had a lot of confidence. When he paid attention to me, something inside me bloomed.

The morning after our first night together, Gene came to band practice with me. The band, which I'd recently joined, was a little like the Mamas and the Papas meets the Fifth Dimension. At least, that's how our eventual record company saw us.

Three girls and two guys: Alan Miles, Jimmy Lott (who, coincidentally, had gone to school with Gene Simmons; it really is a supersmall world), Franny Eisenberg, Carolyn Ray, and me. Alan, Jimmy, and I wrote the material. We had great harmonies, catchy tunes, and Jimmy and I switched off lead vocals. Gene dug it, took us to meet Neil Bogart, president of the label that Kiss was on, Casablanca Records, and Neil signed us. Just like that. On the spot.

So my waitressing job at the Great American manifested itself into my first record deal. It all happened very quickly.

As I remember, we sang for Neil in his office on Sunset Boulevard, a swanky setting for us young hippie musicians, and within the month we were in NYC, recording an album with producers Dave Appell and Hank Medress, who'd had an early hit when his band, the Tokens, released "The Lion Sleeps Tonight."

Before we knew it, the simple tunes that we'd always sung around a piano and an acoustic guitar had been *produced*. They had production values that we weren't even sure matched the way we wanted our music to sound. Our bandleader, Alan, tried steering our ship as close to the simple sound our music was intended to have. However, as sometimes happens, the record-making machine overwhelmed him.

We came out with a pretty good record, not without a lot of pushing back (thanks, Dad, for that lesson), trying to remain true to our sound.

The album was called *Moon over Brooklyn*. We didn't even have a name for the band at mastering. Release date was swiftly approaching, and nothing seemed to fit.

Neil Bogart came up with the idea of calling us "the Group with No Name." I thought it was ridiculous, but who was I to argue? I was twenty-one and my dream of making records was coming true.

It's what I'd always wanted.

It's what I knew I was supposed to do.

So there we were. As part of the marketing campaign, the label released mysterious ads showing the five of us, just our heads, naked shoulders, with a big question mark under the photo. They were released weekly until the record came out, and then that ridiculous name was revealed with the drop of our first single, "Baby Love (How Could You Leave Me)."

We signed with a manager. We put together a touring band and played promotional gigs, some choice TV spots, including *Don Kirshner's Rock Concert*, and a few local gigs.

We got some airplay. But not much.

The label released another single, "Never You Mind," a song I cowrote.

We sold a few records, but not enough to warrant making another one for Casablanca.

We were picked up by Elektra Records. Released one single. And then, through a combination of a lack of record sales and band infighting, we split up.

Meanwhile, Gene and I were an off-and-on thing—at least I thought we were.

Gene was only five years older than me, but he seemed like an *adult*. He was on the straight and narrow. He never smoked pot or even drank alcohol. I'd never met anyone like that in rock 'n' roll. Or anywhere, actually. He was disciplined—a business-man, really. He understood the record business and what it took to be a success. Everything he did, I knew was right. I so looked up to him.

He was like my focused roommate Joanna during *Two Gents*, who worked tirelessly toward her goals. A trait I was in awe of and wasn't able to do, yet.

"You know what? You're going to be a star someday," Gene told me once.

Then he paused.

"But you know what's going to fuck you up?" he continued, staring at me with his big brown eyes that I had fallen for, hard. "Men. You have a tendency to give it all up for a guy. Don't do it."

Gene had a way of making me feel like I was the only girl in the room and on his mind. Despite the hundreds of Polaroids of other women I eventually found in his New York apartment one afternoon, after he'd flown me in to see him. He was always honest about his love of women. I was never foolish enough to think I was the only one.

Sort of.

At twenty-two, without even realizing I was doing it, I fantasized I would be the exception. It took me years to learn when people tell you who they are, believe them.

Around this time, I'd met Freddie Beckmeier, when he'd come to audition for the touring band of TGWNN. Finally believing that Gene was not my one and only, I started dating Freddie. We quickly became an item. When Freddie asked me to marry him, Gene was still on my mind. So I called him.

"Hey, it's Katey," I said, heart in throat. "Freddie asked me to marry him. I'm not sure how to answer. I'll say no if you want to marry me."

Gene laughed.

He knew I had to ask, even though I already knew the answer.

There was that book of Polaroids. I finally had to genuinely accept that I wasn't the only one. And also, that he wasn't going to let me lose myself in him and jeopardize my future. He'd told me not to give it up for a guy.

And I never did. I heeded his lesson. It was invaluable. No matter how much my relationships struggled or cost me, I never let them stop me. I always kept working.

Head in a Bag

I was a chubby tween.

When I was twelve, I had a best friend, a food buddy, who was also kind of chubby.

We went to the Brentwood Country Mart after school, where we used to sneak burgers and fries and milk shakes.

They were forbidden fare for both of us. Looking over our shoulders, nervously expecting to get busted, we dipped the salty fries in the sweet vanilla shakes.

I was supposedly on Weight Watchers or some other diet plan.

I wasn't supposed to cheat. But I always did.

My dad was neither thin nor fat, but he was weight obsessed and constantly on a diet. And when he was dieting, we were all dieting.

My dad became as obsessed with watching my weight as he was obsessed with watching his.

His on-and-off diet whims could change from day to day, but we never questioned him.

We simply dieted, or didn't, as he did.

He loved his latkes and bagels, but when we were dieting, he had a strict rule: no potatoes, no starch. This was before the low-carbohydrate Atkins diet.

It was the grapefruit and cottage cheese era, and we ate a lot of both.

During the times we were forbidden from eating cake and cookies, Dad liked to eat navel oranges for dessert or as a snack before bed.

I peeled oranges for the both of us.

Eating them voraciously together.

The smell of oranges still makes me think of my dad.

When I was a teenager, my father was the one in my family who took me shopping for clothes at Bullock's and Saks department stores. My mother wasn't up for it.

I couldn't fit into anything in the teen department, and I'd always end up in tears, blaming the clothes, blaming the store, blaming my mom.

She assigned my dad the task of daughter dressing.

Mom was a uniform dresser. She'd find one dress that worked and buy four of the same in different colors.

Dressing me became too complicated. Too much for Mom.

My dad and I had to go to the women's department to find my size, where he picked out all these gross women's dresses for me. It was really bad being a teenage girl who had to go shopping with her dad. My mortification was acute.

I rejected the women's department. I started wearing the same pair of baggy jeans every day after that.

Then *his* mortification was acute.

I had no female role models to show me the ways of wardrobe and makeup.

I'd say I got my grandmother's practicality and my mother's heart, which was like getting the best of them both.

But even with all the good stuff I learned from these two matriarchs of my family—how to run the house and master practical concerns, and how to feel deeply—there was so much that neither of them was around to teach me.

There was no role model of femininity; no one to show me what goes where. So I went the other way: a boyish hippie chick in my ripped-up jeans.

For so many years, I could never figure out what I looked like. I couldn't see myself. I was blurry.

I became chameleon-like, morphing into what or who was in my world. Taking on the traits of others, in hopes of bumping into me.

As a result, for years, I thought I was you—a quality that became useful only when I started acting.

The cost of having a mother die too young and a father work too much. There's no one to mirror, and so you don't know how to be or who you are.

*   *   *

My weight obsession is my oldest and most unrelenting companion, my constant conversation, my go-to when something's buggin' me and I need to give a name to what it is. It all turns to "I'm too fat." The catchphrase I used to give name to my sad heart. My default thought. Deeply embedded.

I was fat at the worst time of life to be fat—the years twelve to eighteen—and then "chunky" on and off throughout my twenties, depending on how much speed or cocaine I did.

Things escalated when I was around sixteen years old, and my concerned parents *really* became concerned and forced me to get serious about my growing size. I was no longer just a chubby tween. And "big boned" wasn't cutting it. They woke up to reality before I was ready to hear it.

They finally intervened and forced me to get on a scale and face the facts; verify what I had been denying. "No, I'm not that heavy," I'd say.

When the number smiled back at me—190 pounds—I was overwhelmed by my own lack of awareness. I really had no idea I was 50 pounds overweight.

I'd been totally disconnected from my body.

Where I grew up, the showbiz community, sunny, beachy Los Angeles, to be fat was the worst of the worst things you could be.

So I denied it.

And then faced with my number, I wondered, How could I have not known?

How could my body have deceived me like that?

I thought the scales were lying.

I didn't think I ate that much. And, consciously, I probably didn't. But I was like a blackout drunk with food.

It happened mostly when I came home after school to an empty house. Either my mom was at her psychiatrist—this was back in the day when people literally went in and lay on the couch, and she did that five days a week—or she was in bed, or she was out doing normal Mom things.

We never quite knew.

Whatever she was or wasn't up to, the house always felt empty. Lonely.

And so I went to my room.

I had my own little TV in my room. And I watched TV and I ate.

Oreo cookies, bologna sandwiches on white bread, potato chips.

It wasn't about the food. It was about the eating.

Those hours between three and five in the afternoon are still tough for me. I now no longer want to make food my babysitter, and I'm better at being alone with me now. But when I'm in an empty house, late afternoon, after school hours, before the sun goes down, I feel nervous.

After 190, my sneaking days were over. My parents immediately took me to the doctor, who prescribed a combo of diet pills and diuretics.

It was the beginning of what turned into a fifteen-year addiction to drugs and eventually alcohol.

The diet pills didn't really work.

They helped me lose a little weight, but mostly they made me talk more, made me more social.

I felt happier.

What I probably needed was an antidepressant.

When I look at pictures of myself as a tween it's clear how sad I was.

I was a sad, chubby kid.

Until I was a hyper, slightly less chubby kid, which was better.

Until I was hooked on whatever it took to stay skinny, or at least skinnier, and better wasn't better anymore.

As I see it now, I had become a stuffer: bad feeling, feed it. Explosive situation: suck it up.

Drink it away, smoke screen it, pill pop it.

Stick your head in a bag and keep it there.

When I finally woke up to reality, I engaged in a full-on war. I fought my body with whatever it took to win.

Forget what was healthy.

Forget what my body might actually want, or need.

I would go to any lengths to shrink my size.

I took on my dad's way of thinking about his weight, and became obsessed with managing and controlling my body's size.

I still struggle with his negative voice in my head, which became my own negative voice in my head.

When I was a senior in high school, at seventeen, diet pills escalated to street speed. I'd already started drinking red wine and smoking pot, which was completely the worst thing you can do to lose weight. I liked getting high, and speed allowed me to do both, get high and not overindulge in food.

Plus, cigarettes, lots and lots of cigarettes.

In the mid- to late 1970s, when I was out on my own and supporting myself as a backup singer and musician, speed turned to cocaine, accompanied by vodka (the fewest calories) and any kind of downer narcotic I could muster up to take the edge off.

About five years into my "cure," substances were no longer about shrinking myself. By then, I had to have them. To function.

A hit of something to open my eyes.

Pills and booze to shut me down at night.

I was afraid to let myself know the full force of what I was doing, where I was heading, who I was becoming.

Five years in, drugs and alcohol were what I relied on. An array of substances quieted the negative, fearful voices that would only get louder as the high subsided.

So then there needed to be more medication.

And it worked—as well as it ever does—for the next decade.

My attitude and vigilance about my weight have subsided over the years. Mostly from boredom and a lot of work on (ugh) self-acceptance.

Even after all these years of sobriety, which have helped me to live in a more even, less fearful place, my discomfort with my body is my forever reliable crutch.

When in need, I can point my free-floating anxiety, which has run with me my whole life, at my physical self and give it a place to land.

On a good day, that anxious low rumble is the motivating kind.

I rename it—call it energy or excitement.

But on days when I have nowhere to channel my nerves, it can morph into a body dysmorphic weight preoccupation, where I am always fat, always unlovable, never enough.

If I can find a space from which to intervene in my own thought process and step out of my dark leanings for just a moment, I can usually track my fat eyes to what they are actually gazing on.

Most certainly not anything to do with my size or my body.

Most definitely find a clue, like bread crumbs, leading me to what really is at the source of that pain-filled moment.

Addiction is all about not feeling feelings.

Numbing out.

Blanking out.

Keeping your head in a bag.

Food was the first way I learned to do that.

And even now that I'm finally in my body, and have been for years, there's always the temptation to check out and to put food—or drugs and alcohol—over feelings.

And so I push back.

Feelings over food.

Life over substances.

Pills

When I was twelve, we lived on the same block as Judy Garland.

Her daughter Lorna Luft and I became neighborhood buddies.

Lorna's mom had a lot of pills on her bedside table and slept past noon just like my mom. We hung tight.

And, of course, I thought everyone's mom took a lot of pills.

And then, when I was fourteen, our family doctor prescribed me diet pills, and so I had pills of my own.

I got the message: if you feel bad, take a pill.

And they worked.

But the diet pills did more than make me lose weight.

They gave me a sense of well-being and self-esteem where I'd had none, made me more social and unafraid to take chances, and gave me a way to fix what ailed me.

Along with my pills I used to smoke weed, drop acid, and drink red wine. I remember chatting up with my parents while under the influence like it was no big deal.

I don't think the drugs were quite as strong then, because I could kind of function on them.

I didn't like my mom's pills. She was on heart medication. So many different ones.

It was so weird in those days, how when you had heart disease, they didn't want you to move around too much.

They didn't want you to exercise.

They liked you to stay still.

Calm and medicated.

Unagitated, as that might lead to problems.

If a heart didn't beat too hard, it might last longer.

There was also very little nutritional advice about how to keep a heart healthy, not like there is now. So my mother ate candy and took her pills.

And so when I started smoking pot, which calmed me off my diet pills, my teenage self decided that pot would be a better alternative for my mom, too.

I thought it was the be-all, end-all to everything that ailed ya. And so I tried to get her to smoke.

My mom used to let me have band jam sessions at our family house.

She'd send my dad to a hotel for the night, so we could throw what was essentially a rave. She let me push the furniture aside and set up our band stuff in the living room.

It was one of the few times that I felt a real sense of belonging at my house, being my real self in the vicinity of my family, or at least my mom.

The guys in my band at the time all really liked her.

And the few times I've run into people I knew in high school, they always tell me how much they loved her.

These parties were *the happening thing*, and they thought she was so cool for letting them happen.

My mom was either in her bedroom or in the living room during these jam sessions, sort of in her own world.

It wasn't like she was up cooking snacks; she wasn't *that* mom.

She was "Cool Mom," basking in—not judging—our youthful exuberance.

It was 1970, so she was probably dressed for the occasion in her high-rise blue jeans and a flowy blouse. Still really simple in her appearance, her hair short, with just a little lipstick.

She didn't wear jewelry.

On one of these nights, I had a conversation with Mom about an alternative approach to treating her heart disease. It was one of those times when talking to my mom meant lying down with her, in bed, or on the couch.

So that's what I did, during a jam session.

I stretched out by her side on the couch.

Sensing I had her attention, I made my case.

"You know, Mom, you really should try smoking pot instead of taking all those pills," I said to her. I'm sure I was high at the time.

"I'll think about it," she said.

My mom actually tried pot, but she wasn't with me when she did. She just told me about it later.

"I liked it," she said. "But I couldn't tell your dad."

I got what she meant.

In those days, some parents were smoking pot, but it was much more the cocktail generation.

I always loved to see my mom in the glow of those teenage parties, open, easy and breezy, comfortable, funny.

Watching my friends all gravitate to her light, her wisdom.

As I reflect back now, I'm so grateful that I got to experience that vision of her, but it also made it doubly sad to see her sink when she inevitably did.

In my naïve way, I still believed that she could get better if she wanted to; that it was somehow her choice to remain dulled, to remain sick.

Now I understand all she was up against, and I'm just so glad I got to be with her in her full light for the brief moments when she could be in it herself.

By morning, after our *happening*, the furniture would be back in place, Dad would be back home, and we would be back to who we'd always been.

Hardworking, coming-and-going Dad; Mom tucked away in her room—like our magical mystery tour had never been.

Band Life

When I was growing up, one of my girlfriends had an older sister, Julie, who was a scholar.

"Why can't you be more like Julie?" my dad asked me frequently.

"I'm just not," I said.

For a while, I tried. And then I pushed back. *Fuck that, I'm not like that.*

I liked books too, but not the kind my dad valued. Ram Dass, Hermann Hesse, that was my bag. I wanted my consciousness raised, expanded. Made into someone I wasn't, but not necessarily who he wanted me to be. My father really did communicate in terms of "How many books did you read this week?" I turned to music and made it into my entire world. It was my way of sidestepping altogether the conversation with my dad about what mattered, pretending that I didn't care if I didn't live up to his expectations.

I always thought he loved my brother David best, because he was scholarly and eventually went to Harvard.

I just wasn't that kid.

Looking back, I understand my dad's European-immigrant, Depression-era attitude: you've got to be book smart to make a living in this world. But at the time, I couldn't take it.

And my dad wasn't the only one whose expectations overwhelmed me. Just being a girl was too much. Girls were always worried, it seemed to me—especially about boys, which made me worry even more than I already did about them. It was always so difficult for me to figure out where I fit in with girls. Or if I fit in at all. Teenage girls talked so much. I had trouble jumping into conversation. I wanted to talk about more stuff than just boys, like music and philosophy. And then there was the fact I wasn't a cute one. I was chubby, wore all black, and wanted to be Laura Nyro.

When I was in the seventh grade, I had an emotional breakdown. This was before the dress code in schools changed. Girls couldn't wear pants back then, and I had to wear stockings to school every day—the kind with a garter belt. I'd get so confused about how to dress. What to look like. I was awkward. I could never keep my stockings together. Or myself together. I'd come home with runs every day.

By the end of seventh grade, I was an emotional wreck. For eighth grade, my parents sent me away to the Ojai Valley School, a coed boarding school, with fewer students and less competition about what to wear and who your friends were than at my large public school. I got to wear a uniform, so I didn't have to think about how to dress anymore. And I didn't have to endure stockings. Everybody looked the same. What a relief.

My anxiety ran deeper and flared up brighter than other kids' my age. I felt "less than" about my weight, my looks, my brain. I didn't feel pretty enough or smart enough. I felt like a chubby dim bulb.

I liked having guy friends. They were an easier hang for me because I didn't compare myself with them, like I did with girls. I didn't scrutinize myself, or use them as a barometer, a measuring stick, a way to see myself by comparison. Or, as was most often the case, to tear myself down.

In high school, I started singing and playing guitar in bands, and I was usually the only girl. (In my midtwenties, I played with some killer female musicians, like bassist Jennifer Condos, who later toured and recorded with Don Henley and Stevie Nicks and now works with Ray Lamontagne, and percussionist Debra Dobkin, who went on to play with Bonnie Raitt, Richard Thompson, and Jackson Browne. And that's just to name two, but not so much in those younger years.) Just a bunch of dudes. And me. I liked it that way.

I liked the ease I felt around musicians. They didn't measure themselves by their book smarts or their appearances. Not a lot of chatter about facts and figures. Not a lot of chatter at all. My dad made me feel stupid, but musicians never did. It was more about playing their instruments, and I could do that.

This guy, Tom Virgil, who I knew from Palisades High

School, opened a record store in the middle of town called the Electric America Record Store. We'd all get together in the store's parking lot and have jam sessions. We covered songs like Traffic's "Dear Mr. Fantasy" and "Love the One You're With" by Stephen Stills. I don't know whether we were any good or not, but I thought we were great. Sometimes it would turn into a party, sometimes just a chance to play.

In the band, I was invited.

I was included.

I was appreciated.

I never felt intimidated.

I was the only girl invited to join in.

So I felt special.

My bandmates were mostly like brothers to me, with an occasional exception for a sexual interlude. It was the seventies, so with the availability of birth control pills, there was a lot of casual sex. Emotionally, I ran extremely deep. So "casual sex" with my music buds felt safer to me. More like an extension of playing music than an affair of the heart—because true romance contained the potential for heartbreak, and my heart broke easily. I'd learned to toughen up around my family: How to not be so dramatic. And that it wasn't always appropriate to show how deeply I felt things. "Shut it down, Sarah Bernhardt," my father used to say.

So I adopted a cool, aloof attitude.

The beginning of a long-term disconnect from my feelings, it was another way of keeping my head in the bag.

Solitary by nature, I've always needed a lot of space. I like room to roam in all my relationships, particularly romantic ones. Not like a cheater, just space to breathe.

To feel myself.

To hear *my* voice, not everyone else's.

I felt so suffocated growing up, by all the big people and their big problems. And their need for me to be a certain way. I needed a door to shut, and this desire for my own space has continued even now, as a big person myself. Guys who love their guitars first and have spent years alone in a room with that first love get that. And that's where I'd been, too: in my room, with my guitar and my piano, making up songs, living other lives through these songs, focused and alone.

As I wasn't much for small talk, playing music did not require much conversation and was simpler for me. I could feel close. I spent many years of my youth and into my twenties in living rooms and eventually rehearsal spaces and concert halls, surrounded by amps and instruments.

And guys speaking that language: amp talk, gear comparisons, lick exchanges, and the wordless communication of playing music. It hits at the heart and has always quieted my brain. My young, very busy brain that never quite knew where to land always found safe haven with the guys in the band. In a room filled with music so loud you can't talk over it, I found calm.

It would drown out the chatter in my head.

And music is still my preferred world of refuge. It's always where I wander when in doubt. It is my most familiar ground.

It's very hard to describe the feeling of playing music.

I share music with my children now. Both of my older kids are musicians. They're amazing, musical, soulful kids. They both make me better as a musician. When I see their natural joy in music, they help me to remember what it feels like to play. We all play together. It's peaceful. True intimacy, for me, was first born in the bond of playing music with people.

Needing to Be Needed

My first boyfriend was a man of few words, but he played a standup bass. So who needed to talk? He was Italian American, long and lanky, dark and brooding, with Mick Jagger lips and brown hair that hung over one eye. When I was a sophomore in high school, he was a senior. When he transferred in at the beginning of senior year, he seemed out of place—and much older than the other kids—at my WASPy high school, just as I felt out of place. But he didn't seem to care, which drew me to him. I zeroed in on him. I figured my way in was to relate to him through music and to make myself useful, since I didn't think of myself as very attractive. After all, I was chunky and didn't look good in a miniskirt. And I was certain I couldn't be my true, authentic self with him. (If I even knew who that was at fifteen and a half.) He'd never like me then.

So I'd buy him something to eat during lunch period. I'd

offer him a ride home. (I was driving illegally with my learner's permit.) I'd sing him a song. I ultimately threw myself at him. He took the bait. And I believe he started to really like me. One night in the parking lot of his Venice Beach apartment building, the evening mist fogged my car windows, and he wrote sweetly, "I love you," in the condensation before he went upstairs to his apartment. I was gobsmacked. We started hanging out together almost every day after school.

He wasn't in a band with me. But I brought my guitar over to his place, and we played on the street, and he pounded a park bench for percussion. We opened my guitar case and played for whatever people threw in. I grew up in the wealthiest part of Los Angeles, but I kept that to myself. I felt embarrassed by my affluence, living in Brentwood, so I didn't invite him over. I went down to Venice Beach and sang for money on the street. That was cool for me. I let him keep the money. I didn't need it.

He had his own apartment. His mom lived on the top floor of his Brooks Avenue building, and he had his own place one floor below with a living room, and a bedroom. In time, we ended every afternoon in his bed, going a little further each day. When his mom would come down and knock on the door, I'd hide in the closet until she went away.

Finally, feeling safe, I gave myself up to him. I loved that guy. He was my first, and the one I opened my heart to, as well as everything else. Almost instantly after we finally crossed the line, he broke up with me with no explanation. There were no more rides home. There was no more passing the hat on Venice Boardwalk. I was devastated. I got the message that I wasn't enough, but I didn't know why. Maybe it was because I was not so hot. Or maybe I hadn't given enough. I needed to be more helpful. Give sex quicker. Be better at sex.

His rejection set up a pattern that made me push harder in those ways. Instead of interpreting our breakup from a healthy perspective—*Maybe if I had gotten to know him better, taken time, he would have really fallen for the real me in a deep way*—I got the message that the way into finding love was to hide myself, buy it, or to have sex with it—quickly and often—and that was all. So distorted. Poor sixteen.

For the next five years, I gave away my body frequently, in hopes of finding love.

I met Freddie Beckmeier, my first husband, when I was twenty-two, and he came to audition for the Group with No Name. Another tall, lanky bass player. I always liked the rhythm section. Soulful Freddie, the bass man, was from Philadelphia and had come up listening to, and eventually playing, soul music. All that wonderful music—Otis Redding, Al Green, and producer-arranger-songwriters (Kenny) Gamble, (Leon) Huff, and (Thom) Bell—came to me through Freddie. I already had a pretty extensive, knowledgeable love of blues, but I was not as familiar with the music that held his heart. He opened my eyes and ears to soul.

From the first time he walked into the rehearsal hall where we were auditioning, I swooned a little. He was aloof and handsome, just like I liked. I was in a power position—this was my band; he was a hired gun—and that was where I found my confidence: wanting a cover for my real self and her inherent vulnerabilities, needing to be needed, having something to offer. Even though my amphetamines had finally shrunk me so I was looking pretty good, I believed, once again, that just me wasn't enough. This time I didn't buy him lunch or give him rides. I gave him a job. And, quickly, sex.

At the time Freddie auditioned for my band, he was also plugging into the LA session scene and playing gigs with the amazing Etta James. "Miss Etta," as we liked to call her, was not only Freddie's employer, but also she had kind of adopted him—as well as all the guys in her band—into her family. She was always surrounded by family. Her career was in a precarious place at that time. Having been at the top of the charts in the 1950s and early 1960s, this legendary singer was still releasing records, but was struggling to stay relevant, as most of the authentic blues artists were at that time. Her husband was her tour manager, her son Donto, just a kid at the time, was always at gigs and always on the bus. Her other son, Sametto, stuck close too. In hard times, she showed me, family sticks together.

From the start of our relationship, I clung to Freddie. In hindsight, I was desperately looking for a place to land. My mom had died the year before I met him, and I barely remember the year that followed. And so I didn't think twice about moving in with him almost immediately. At the same time, I became a part of Etta's family.

It was also an uncertain time for me musically. The Group with No Name drifted apart in 1978, and suddenly I was a singer for hire: recording publishing demos, songs for songwriters trying to get material to a specific artist, occasional sessions as a backup singer, a jingle date. I went to an open audition with 250 other female singers to be a backup singer for Bette Midler, her "Staggering Harlettes."

I made the cut down to 100, and then, down to 25. I eventually got hired. That was a pretty big deal, and just in the nick of time, as I wasn't sure what was next. Now I had a regular gig. I went on the road with Bette intermittently leaving Freddie and his musical family behind. Unbeknownst to me then, the lessons I learned while with Bette would be invaluable to me for the rest of my life.

Being one of Bette's "Staggering Harlettes," or being a chorus girl in a Broadway show, or even doing a ninety-nine–seat equity waiver musical in some shit hole back alley converted garage, were all the same lesson.

Theater folks are no joke.

They know how to show up.

But these lessons were really driven home for me when I worked with Bette, a gal with serious theatrical chops. That was truly one of the hardest jobs I think I've ever had. When I backed Bette, I traveled all over the world, doing the same show, night after night. And yet, four to five days a week, she would hold rehearsals, to run a number, in the lobby of our hotel. Her dedication taught me so much about discipline and work ethic.

I watched her, night after night, sing the same song over and over again, and do it like she'd never done it before. She could tell the same jokes a dozen nights in a row, and they'd still be funny. She could make people cry at the same point every night. Authentic tears motivated by her genuine performance. It was a theatrical approach, and she was a master. I'd grown up in a showbiz family but suddenly saw with new eyes how much work it required. That was a huge lesson for me. Bette had a more extensive theater background, and I identified more as a musician in the band. It was better than any theater school I could have gone to, in terms of learning serious artistry and professionalism.

Bette and I always related on a musical level and on an emotional level. Our sensitivities kind of matched. Some people who worked with her matched her cutting wit. But I was a little bit crumbly, not that cynical. She liked that soft side of me, as I recognized the soft side of her. She reminded me of my dad in so many ways because she could be tough, but she was also so squishy inside.

During my early years with Bette, when I'd go home to Freddie, that meant going deeper into Etta's family. Miss Etta's band had its share of late-night jam sessions at our place, and she was a frequent visitor to our rustic Laurel Canyon house on the corner of Lookout Mountain Road and Horseshoe Canyon. I'd lived there a few years before with my bandmate, singer Mindy Sterling. Because it had a turret, we'd dubbed it "the Castle." Now I was living in it again with my fiancé, Freddie. Boozy, weed and coke filled, late into the night, there was a lot of music played there. That's where Etta first heard me sing, handing me the mic and giving me the nod, in the living room. Maybe it was "Further on Up the Road," a Bobby "Blue" Bland tune. Or some old Muddy Waters thing. Whatever it was, I thought, *I know that song. I'm going to fucking open my mouth and sing with Etta James. Yikes!*

I stood close to Freddie, who'd always encouraged me and made me feel safe musically. Who was the coolest cat I knew, and who wouldn't have let me be involved in all this if he thought I didn't have the chops. So weird: by this time, I'd made two records, sung numerous times on television and on stages around the country, sung in front of hundreds, maybe thousands, of people, and gotten some nice pats on the back; yet standing in our living room with one of the greatest singers of our time, I thought for sure that nothing would come out of my mouth.

I closed my eyes, took the mic, timidly opened my mouth, and I sang.

One verse, and then another, somebody soloed, another verse, and then I passed the mic back and slowly opened my eyes.

Etta James was smiling at me.

That look of camaraderie, from one musician to another, her sly grin and slow nod as she acknowledged, "Wow, girl can *saa-ang*."

It meant so much to me.

My favorite singers coming up had all been black: Aretha Franklin, Nina Simone, Ella Fitzgerald, Etta James. And I always secretly wished I was a black girl singer. I was always drawn to the emotion, the tone, the rhythm of black music. Even my white girl idols sang like black chicks: Laura Nyro, Janis Joplin, and Tracy Nelson of Mother Earth and Cold Blood's Lydia Pense, two of my faves from the late 1960s San Francisco music scene.

So to have Miss Peaches wrap me up in her arms and whisper in my ear, "You go, girl"— well, it's up there with my top five moments of all time. Three of those being the births of my children.

She provided a different kind of musical education from Bette, as well as becoming kind of a motherly figure. She asked me about my relationship with Freddie, gave me sound advice when I asked for it—and, in her sweet way, even when I didn't, because she knew I needed it. She appeared to be tough and full of bravado. But on the inside, she was intuitive and caring. In hindsight, I think she saw right through my tough-girl stance. She could see my need to be loved and needed. Etta was thrilled for us when I told her that he'd proposed after we'd been dating for less than a year. A proposal that happened in my parents' bedroom, the one my mother had slept in. Since her death, I'd become a frequent presence at home, when no one was there, just to feel close to her. Freddie would come with me, and in my raw state, I'd now let him see where I came from—the me I'd previously hidden behind my boho poor-artist pose. It was striking how quickly after seeing my roots he decided I was the one. I was never really sure if it was me or where I came from that put that ring on my finger. Not exactly a strong endorsement for authenticity making me feel any better about myself.

When I wasn't on the road with Bette, I was, again, a singer for hire. I was available, I was cheap, and I could really sing, plus I was Freddie's girl. Etta offered me a job as her backup singer.

"Really, no shit, unbelievable. *Me???*" I said.

I would be the only girl in the band besides Etta, and the only band member that just sang. Bobby Martin, the keyboard player, also sang, as did Brian Ray, Etta's guitar player during that time, who has now been with Paul McCartney's band for fifteen years. But Etta and I were the only designated singers. Wild.

I did a few tours with Etta, playing all kinds of venues. Shitty dive bars, dinner theaters, rock clubs. When we had small shows in the middle of the country, she had me open the show for her. I came out, sang a song, and then she was the main act. Well, after we'd been on tour awhile, she started getting tired, and she'd have me sing two songs, three songs, four songs, before her set. Pretty amazing, that she let me open the show for her.

The single most memorable gig to me was when we played the Anaheim Stadium, opening for the Rolling Stones. They were playing two nights in a row, and Etta was their request as an opening act. It was surreal, standing onstage, looking out into an audience that big, like I was looking at a poster of a crowd gathered.

All of us, the whole band and Miss Etta, traveled across the country in a single bus with a bedroom in the back for the star to rest up and change her clothes. It was a pretty bare bones operation, as I remember, and us gals shared the bedroom dressing room more than a few times, pulling into whatever small-town venue we'd be playing that night, and passing on the skimpy club accommodations to put on our show clothes, do our hair, paint our faces.

I loved singing with her.

I loved being around her.

The simplicity of her approach.

Etta never oversang. She respected the song and gave emphasis to the notes that were written, rather than adding runs and licks just for the sake of showing off that she could. It's a lesson I've carried.

Less is more, be it a piece of music or a scene to be acted.

Make the simple choices.

If the writing is good, they are there to be made.

Don't add shit.

Don't be a show-off.

* * *

In so many ways, these were my father's lessons, too. But I couldn't see the similarities growing up. As I can see clearly now, my dad also kept it simple. He worked hard and preached humility, probably as a result of growing up poor and an immigrant. And when I did finally grow into my authentic self, I would take so many of his core principles as my own, and with pride.

I don't like the light to shine too brightly on me, either. Now, I can celebrate my accomplishments, a job well done, my joy—not very easily with someone else, not necessarily shouting it from the rooftops, but I can quietly acknowledge them to myself. As a young person, though, I was still figuring out who I was and which of my father's lessons to take as my own. The lesson of humility has clearly stuck.

My father had remarried a little more than a year after my mom died, and he and my stepmother, Marge Champion, of Marge and Gower Champion fame, threw themselves into planning my wedding to Freddie on May 1, 1977. They would have it in the backyard of their home in Brentwood, California, a beautiful Monterey Colonial home my dad had moved the family into after they married. Marge, who was a more patrician addition to the family and not at all versed in the lefty boho leanings of my parents, wanted my nuptials announced in the society column of the *Los Angeles Times*. I allowed them to indulge in the glitz of the wedding, knowing my dad needed to try to fill the hole of my mom's absence for both of us. But I put my foot down at the wedding announcement. Celebrity and society columns were not a part of my upbringing or how I wanted to live now.

Under the tutelage of Marge's blue-blooded patronage, my wedding was a beautiful but very formal, very proper home wedding. The day's biggest moment wasn't when I walked down the aisle. It was the arrival of Etta and her crew.

Suddenly I wanted to hide the big house. I wanted to hide the swimming pool. At age twenty-three, I wore my badge of "struggling artist" very comfortably. And the affluence surrounding my family rubbed up against all that, glaringly, when my "now" life showed up there. I'd always hid the Westside from those outside my family's world.

And then, in the midst of the string quartet at the entrance, food stations with cuisine from around the world, proper tents with tablecloths, place cards, and cloth napkins, there was Etta, her family, and her band. Their large party arrived at the wedding wearing their Sunday best, which for the musicians was sharkskin suits, panama hats, and blue suede shoes.

They were definitely a different vibe from my parents' crowd. I thought for a moment that Etta's band might feel awkward at my wedding. But true to what they had taught me, people are just people. If there had been any unease, it was quickly diffused by my father's warm welcome and reverence for Miss Etta being in his home. After all, he was the reason I had the idols I did, Etta being one of them.

My dad cared about art, not status. He had moved his family to Brentwood when he could afford to, but he didn't expect others to express their success in the same way. Appreciative of the arts more than the trappings of success, my parents understood the ups and downs of an artist's life and had no judgment about them. They'd had plenty themselves when I was little. Before there was success. Before overwork. Before illness. We lived in a one-bedroom apartment in Hollywood. My mom had worked and helped support her family since she was eleven. Singing, writing, script supervising, assistant directing. My dad had been dirt poor and working hard all his life.

At my age, and while still finding my own place in the world and where my value came from, I was probably more worried about the surfaces than he was. My family's artsy backstory—the one so close to my heart and who I was trying to be in my own life—was not something anyone would ever have known from the looks of my wedding. Not the nine times my family had moved over the years, depending on income, as our family expanded and my father continued to build his reputation. Not the fact that my family had landed in this affluent community only as the result of my dad working his ass off.

I was prideful about my independence.

And now, my secret was revealed.

It was almost like when I was a kid, and I wore those ripped jeans and ran off to Venice Beach to busk on the street with my boyfriend, I didn't want anyone to know there was a Lincoln Continental in the garage at home. The lifestyle I'd grown up in didn't justify the blues I was feeling and loved to sing. I'd had plenty of pain and struggle in my childhood to make me relate to the blues. But you couldn't necessarily see that from the outside of my childhood. When I sang, I could share my secret self that had been devalued in my parents' eyes. Maybe Etta saw that, too. I felt exposed because she was now seeing the secret I'd kept from her world. My two worlds, my two selves, had collided, and it was a shock to my system. As soon as the wedding was over, I went back to how I'd been living, taking no parental handouts, neither in the form of love nor money.

Even though I gave Freddie everything I thought he needed, that marriage didn't last more than a few years. But its unraveling didn't teach me about my own self-worth as much as singing with Etta and Bette had. I kept trying to assign my value by what I could give rather than by who I was. In hindsight, they provided the first in a long line of lessons about how it was possible to be accepted for just who I was, but it would be years before I learned that I could be enough without needing to be needed.

The Lump in My Throat

Cue my wakeup call.

Only it didn't wake me up at all.

I found a lump on the side of my throat while checking myself out in the rearview.

Not looking for lumps, just putting on lipstick.

I thought it might be a vocal node. Singers get those, and singing was how I paid the rent in those days. Newly divorced, I wasn't on the road as much. I was sticking to my own music and had become kind of a local LA bar band celebrity.

Twenty-eight years old.

I went to the doctor to show him my lump.

I wasn't really scared, but it was enough to get me to the doctor.

My recollection is that the next day, maybe even that afternoon, I was admitted to Cedars-Sinai Medical Center, eighth floor, cancer ward.

My family doctor, Dr. Kadish, one of those doctors who always looked old even though he probably hadn't been when I'd started seeing him as a kid, approached my situation with the usual blasé tone of voice he always had.

So used to my family and all its calamities, he could have been ordering dinner, just the same as checking me into the hospital.

"Probably a malignancy. (Pass the salt.) Your mom had one. (What's for dessert?) Let's go check it out."

But he also knew bad things did happen in my family.

The "What is the worst-case scenario?" question had been answered with the worse-case scenario more than once.

Just the year before I noticed my lump, my father was killed in a freak accident.

My mother had been found dead in her bed just six years before that.

Growing up, our family spent our share of time in emergency rooms for routine stitches and broken bones (my brothers), and heart attack scares and suicide attempts (my mom).

After my folks passed, Dr. Kadish took on the five of us kids as best as he could, in terms of our general health and checkups.

Dr. Kadish, grumpy old Arnold Kadish, the doctor who swore my mother died of a heart attack but never performed an autopsy. And left me to wonder if she'd assisted herself out the exit door.

He said it was my thyroid.

That we'd have to open me up and have a look.

That my mother had had the same lump in her throat when she was my age.

Hers was cancer. He knew my mother's health history.

It can be hereditary. Or not.

Even if mine was cancer too, he said it wasn't a big deal. We'd remove it and be done with it.

(I was kind of happy to have something else in common with my mom. Well, sort of.)

When my mother had the operation, she suffered nerve damage to her vocal cords, and the Singing Sweetheart of Cherokee County could never sing again.

That made me nervous.

"Be careful because I'm a singer," I told the surgeon.

The possibility of having cancer didn't even really compute, but losing my voice did.

At twenty-eight, I thought I was immortal.

Plus, in those days, cancer was the taboo, whispered C-word.

I'd never heard of it happening to young people, besides my mom. It happened to old people, and that wasn't me.

So I was sure it wasn't cancer.

The surgery itself was super fast.

I was wrong. It was cancer, but they got it all.

I didn't have any parents, so there was no spare room to curl up in. My boyfriend at the time brought me home from the hospital to my place in Venice and dropped me off.

All I had to do for aftercare was to drink this radiated iodine. For twenty-four hours, no one could be around me.

As soon as it was all over, I went out to the backyard to smoke.

There was no one to take care of me, so I pretended there was nothing serious to take care of.

My denial system was finely attuned by this point, and I could deny severity, joy, reality, fear.

I could deny anything.

So I just did what I knew how to do.

When you lose your parents young and there's no one to run home to, so you either minimize things, or you go crazy. Because there's no place to put anything you feel; anything that happens to you.

And for me, I continued drinking and drugging everything away.

That helped me to minimize.

I would sort of numb out.

My lump had been removed, along with the whole thyroid (definitely cancer).

"If you are going to have cancer, this is the kind to get." That's what my doctor said.

I went to a psychic healer who made the connection between cancer in the throat and the inability to express anger.

So curious: my mother and me, both of us rageful young women, having had lumps of disease in our throats.

My sad, sweet, disappointed mom. Not able to be who she really was.

She was mad, and she put a cork in it.

Me? Well, my dad had recently been killed. That pissed me off. Just as I was finally getting to know the guy. Just as I was finally not afraid of him. Just as his softer, sweeter, older side started to emerge, he was gone.

And that made me really mad.

The surgery was successful, but I did have nerve damage—my biggest fear, realized. For six months, I couldn't sing at all.

That got my attention. It freaked me out.

And yet it didn't stop me from smoking. It didn't stop me from drinking.

In hindsight, though, I realize a seed was planted.

Within the next three years, I got sober.

I was really concerned about my voice, because that's how I made my living. And that's what I loved. I was heart-broken to not be able to sing. I made my vocal recovery a priority.

For six months, I had serious vocal therapy three times a week, intensive vocalizing that was like physical therapy for your vocal chords.

The doctors had told me that my voice would probably come back, but no one could give me 100 percent reassurance.

My band at the time played with other people and took other gigs, but they let me know they'd be there when I was ready to work again.

My welcome-back gig was at Madame Wong's West, a

Chinese restaurant with a showcase room in the back, in Santa Monica. Since owner Ester Wong had begun showcasing bands, including the Ramones and The Knack, there at night in the late 1970s because business was bad, she'd become known locally as the "godmother of punk rock."

Everyone was there for my return gig: my patron of the arts, Johnny Starbuck; Jay Gruska and Paul Gordon; Sarah Taylor; all my musical cohorts at the time.

There was tension in the air until I nailed my first notes and everyone cheered.

I was back. One hundred percent.

As soon as I was able, I also returned to the road, resuming my regular life as a backup singer for Bette Midler and whoever else would hire me.

I still wasn't digesting the whole experience.

I still wasn't in my body.

My cancer was a wake-up call about the fragility of my voice. But nothing else.

My addictions won out, as they always do. Drugs and alcohol made it possible for me to continue on as if nothing had happened.

I'd been mad and disappointed for years, but if you asked me, I'd say I was fine. Always "fine."

I'd like to say that having cancer started me on a journey of deep exploration and excavation into the root of my rage, but that didn't really happen, either.

In those years, I still had my head in a bag, even if it was a different bag.

A few years later, when I got sober, I had to buddy up to that angry kid who was running the show—had to let her speak—because she finally got too loud to contain.

Everyone Needs a Johnny Starbuck and Other Angels on the Way to Here

I won a Golden Globe Award in 2011 for the role of Gemma Teller Morrow on *Sons of Anarchy*.

I'm really proud of it. I'd been nominated five previous times for my Peg on *Married with Children*, but never won. It was satisfying to finally win, and it was way better than not winning. Being nominated is, truthfully, not as good as winning.

Every acceptance speech I've ever heard, as well as the few I've given, thanks the people along the recipient's career path who have done the heavy lifting, often behind the scenes, creating and supporting opportunity, usually without receiving any recognition of their own. I've had some heavy lifters on my road. Like Johnny Starbuck.

I met Johnny for the first time in 1974. I was living in Laurel Canyon. Life there was simple. Modest bungalows and log cabins nestled between washed-out mansions left over from the time when Hollywood's silent-movie stars lived there. The canyon felt like its own world. An artistic haven for anyone, artistic or not. Actually, no one really went to Laurel Canyon, or knew about it, unless they lived there. Even better. Plus, the music I loved to listen to came out of the quiet canyon. So naturally I wanted to live there too.

My roommate at the time, Mindy Sterling, had a boyfriend named Snuffy Walden, who was the lead guitarist in a rock band called Stray Dog. Johnny Starbuck was its roadie. Mindy and I had met while waitressing at the Great American Food and Beverage Co., the restaurant where we simultaneously waited on tables and entertained the diners. We both shared the dream of singer-songwriter stardom and decided to combine our voices and writing skills into a duo called Sterling Silver, which we were convinced would head straight to the top of the charts.

We were well matched: naïve, enthusiastic, and tenacious. Laurel Canyon was the place for two young singer-songwriters, wannabe "Ladies of the Canyon." And we were good. We wrote some substantial tunes, our voices a great blend of pop and soul, and became kind of local up-and-comers. We played around, were courted by everyone from Kim Fowley (the six-foot-five Svengali behind the all-girl band The Runaways) to Paul Rothchild (producer of The Doors, Janis Joplin, and Joni Mitchell), and were put in the studio by several labels, including A&M Records, to make demos, always with a record deal on the horizon.

Mindy and I lived in the Castle, the house on the corner of Lookout Mountain Road and Horse Shoe Canyon Road, where I later lived with my husband Freddie, two doors up from where Joni Mitchell had lived when she wrote a slew of beautiful music, and around the corner from Frank Zappa's legendary house in the canyon. The turret was my room, a circular bedroom on the top floor, overlooking the Hollywood Hills.

It would become a house that many phases of my young life walked through. When Mindy and I first rented it, there were three of us of girls living there. I can't remember what we paid, but it was affordable, split three ways. Somehow we always made rent while maintaining our musical pursuits; passing a hat at our gigs, getting the occasional songwriter demo session where we were asked to perform a songwriter's material in the style of the artist they hoped would record it, and waitressing when and where our weak skills would be tolerated. Writing music in whatever time was left.

I was then, as I am now, seriously committed to the only thing I had a skill set for: being an artist. I know how that sounds. Kind of snooty. But what I mean is, I never had a plan B. It was this or . . . what? In my years of struggling, I did think to myself, *If something doesn't happen soon—if some door doesn't swing open so I can actually start making a living—I guess I could try selling real estate. I love houses, so I might be good at that; get my picture on a bus bench.* But I never went so far as to make a serious plan to do that. The bell rang just in time, so I never had to.

Anyway, Johnny Starbuck started showing up at all our gigs. He had maybe five or six years on me, but he seemed much older than that. Like a grown-up had finally appeared in my chaotic young life. With wisdom. And patience.

Johnny Starbuck became a fan of our music and had a huge crush on Mindy (from afar; she was Snuffy's), as most guys did in those days. Mindy was young, blonde, and hot. Unlike me: kind of dark, sad, and not so hot.

Johnny and Snuffy used to show up at the Castle, and while Snuffy and Mindy were locked behind a bedroom door, Johnny and I drank coffee and smoked cigarettes in the kitchen. We became close friends, and at a certain point, he became our third roommate.

Johnny dug the music Mindy and I made together. But when our duo ended, with Mindy being courted away into a solo project, and me getting the gig singing behind Bette Midler as one of her Harlettes, his attention remained focused on me as a solo artist.

Johnny was—still is—chiseled-jaw handsome. He had stubble before it was cool and an outlaw quality about him. Long and lean. I can still see him moving to the beat of the reggae music he loved to listen to, spliff in hand, shades on indoors. A cool cat. He rode a Harley. Johnny Starbuck is not his real name. He made it up, 'cos he didn't like his real one.

He also was and still is a musician, without actually being one. A true music lover with an intense record collection and knowledge. An archivist of great music. He understands the language of rock 'n' roll and plays a mean air guitar.

Johnny was a Renaissance man and kind of an anarchist—not in an angry way, but a freethinker. He lived the existential belief that "nothing really means anything anyway, so why worry or give anything weight?" I had been obsessed with Alan Watts in

high school, and the way Johnny philosophized about life reso-
nated with me just as Alan Watts had. He was like a Buddhist
before I knew what that was. Over the years, he would show himself to be a kind of Zen master. Unattached, nothing was a problem, only an opportunity.

Johnny and I formed a partnership. He became my unofficial
manager. I'd sing; he took care of the rest.

I was doing a showcase for a label at Club Lingerie, a now-
defunct local hang on Sunset Boulevard, littered with wannabe
recording artists, like me, and the record company A&R folks
who trolled after them, looking for artists to sign to the label.
The club had a familiar stank of beer and cigarettes, wall-to-
wall red carpeting that squished underfoot, and an open dance
floor in front of the stage, lined by red vinyl booths that stuck to
you when you slid in. It was a room I'd sung in many times, but
tonight the heat was on: a record company was in the crowd to
see me. Johnny wrangled our gear onstage, helped me keep my
composure, knocked back a few with me.

"I'm fucking freaked out," I said. "I can't stop thinking about
them being here. Don't tell me where they're sitting."

"Yeah, me too," he said. "I got butterflies—feels like excitement. I'm gonna call it that: excitement."

That's how he handled things. That was his gift to me: perspective, reframing, courage in the face of possible rejection.
And love. He loved me, and what I did, and believed everyone
else would too.

Turns out, the record company A&R people there that night
liked me, and before they knew if it was love, they wanted to meet

me. For lunch; how corporate. And just me, not with Johnny or my official manager at the time, Ron Weisner, who managed Paul McCartney, Michael Jackson, Madonna, and little ol' me. I had to show up by myself. I decided to wear my best jumpsuit with my largest shoulder pads, cinched at my waist with elastic, and some smokin' hot white boots.

A couple days after the lunch, they passed.

Was it my outfit? I actually wondered.

Once again, I'd gotten so close to a solo record deal, but it hadn't happened. The story of my life at that time. I was always an almost!

I was sitting on my bed in the turret at the Castle, dejected and rejected, sobbing on my Indian print bedspread, knowing for sure that no one would ever let me make a solo record. The beat of Johnny's reggae music vibrated the floor, and the song he played over and over again, Third Worlds' reggae version of "Now That We Found Love," lifted my head. Johnny stood at my door, looking at me quietly.

"Kate, it's gonna be okay," he said, using the name only my closest friends use. "God's rejection is God's protection. Fuck 'em, let's keep going."

And we did.

He meant so much to me. Johnny gave me what my family never could. It still astounds me that I was able to receive it. With a stoic yet positive energy that could calm the most anxious musician, he derived his own sense of self from helping artists achieve their vision. Be it loading and carrying gear for up-and-comers like Stray Dog or, ultimately, the Rolling Stones. Or what he eventually ended up doing for my career and me: paying my rent when I couldn't make it, covering my bills and band expenses, paying for studio time so I could record—anything he could do to support my talent and get it recognized.

We weren't romantic. We were closer than that. Romance would have fucked up things. And gotten in the way of what we actually were to each other. He derived pride and significance from involving himself in what I was creating. My music became a "we" creation. Choosing songs, finding players, booking gigs—we made all those decisions together.

A patron of the arts? Absolutely. If it hadn't been for the time, encouragement, and hard cash that Johnny threw my way during those years, what has come to me might still have been. But there is a more than good chance my world never would have spun in such a creatively lucrative way.

I was no slouch during those years, and I didn't take advantage of our partnership. I worked hard, writing, recording, gigging, but Johnny arranged things so that I had the luxury of focusing on the music alone whenever I got off the road.

I was always happy for the work I had touring at that time, but felt frustrated that I wasn't fronting the band. He helped me hold that dream; always made me feel I was on the right track. He even produced and carried the financial load of a musical, *Backstreet*, that two of my friends wrote. Acting in that show ultimately got me discovered by my agent and started me on the road to a serious acting career. One to which we (myself included) all responded: "Who knew she could do *that*?"

* * *

Even before we finally reconciled in 2011, I never knew if I'd thanked Johnny enough for those early years. When suddenly my world switched gears, and I became a working actor, my music had to take second position and our "us" started to fade. In all the rush of my new love, acting, I don't think I realized the impact it had on him. Me, moving on; our dream, changing colors. We had no formal agreements, I think because we both thought we would never end. We would just continue banging on doors until one of them opened! Neither of us counted on the fact that I'd find a day gig that actually became a passion, and for a while at least, I had to dim the light on my music.

Johnny, in his sweet way, swore his investment in me was never about the money. It was about the art. And even though it was important for me to eventually make good on the money he had invested, I still believe it was always for love and art, for both of us. Commerce was secondary to the support we provided for each other.

I never could have guessed that my music—my primary focus—would take a backseat. After all, it was me, it was how I identified myself. And wherever there was music, there was Johnny. But we came to an end. And that was awkward. Every important musical decision of the previous eleven years of my life had been made with Johnny Starbuck.

My life needed to change at that juncture, right on the cusp of becoming an actress. I only knew it after the fact, though; I didn't realize it at the time. Clarity came only in retrospect. And everything changed so rapidly, I felt almost more like a spectator than a participant.

My new career path followed close behind my finding sobriety. My first TV series, the *Mary* show, which aired during the 1985–86 season, was a testament to the stress and hardship of living the double life of an addict and a working actor. Right after that job, which I could barely show up for, and thanks to the sweet influence of one of that show's stars, I ended up in the recovery rooms. For me to continue on the road that had suddenly opened to me as an actress, I needed to end my double life. I needed to get clean and sober.

My recovery asked more of me than that I merely stop drinking and using. It required a change of the company I kept; the club life and road life I lived. For a while, I had to steer clear of any reminders or temptations from the places and people I was now turning my back on.

Including my music.

When I'm honest, I think my first love had slowly morphed into a desire for the lifestyle more than the sound. My late nights, the ones I insisted I kept in order to write and record, were more and more about giving me reason to cop drugs and chase them down with cocktails.

It all had to go.

I was so sensitive to drugs and alcohol in my early sobriety that if I'd even had a cocktail or two with you once or twice, I couldn't be around you at all lest I feel the draw of getting high. And Johnny Starbuck was a reminder of that place in my life— sometimes a participant, more often than not a guardian. He, sadly, had to go for a while, too.

Married with Children came along two months into my for-real sobriety, begun August 6, 1986. All I could do was hold on for dear life. Having never worked 100 percent clean and sober, I was terrified. I'd turned my back on all I'd known, even my stalwart friend Johnny.

Our relationship faded in 1989. He had helped me more than almost anyone else in my career, and then we had almost no contact for twenty years—until, eight or nine years ago, we unexpectedly lost a close mutual friend from the inner circle of late-night club rats we'd run around with in the seventies and eighties. I went to the service, and there he was: the same old Johnny. He looked great, still handsome, as if he'd been untouched by the years, aside from a little gray at his temples.

I was so happy to see him. But he wouldn't even meet my eyes, and he left without saying hello or good-bye. It was awful. Heartbreaking.

I'd heard through the grapevine that he was upset with me about how our unique relationship had ended, even though I'd believed we'd had thorough emotional and financial closure.

Knowing that someone was so angry at me—and not just anyone, but a person I loved so deeply—I knew I needed to make it right. I tracked down an email address, reached out, and asked the questions I knew would be uncomfortable for him to answer, because in his loving way, he thought I should have known how the separation of us had left him with such a gaping hole, and his feeling that our closure had never been complete.

He made it clear, and I made it right.

And now we have a relationship again. We can speak, and recollect together, which is priceless. That's how important amends are.

Even today, knowing that Johnny and I are in a good place, I feel my heart pound as I bring him up, as I write his name, as

I remember how he loved me, unconditionally, and only wanted me to have what I wanted for myself. I wonder if he knows that is the real gift he gave me. He taught me what love is. And it was a lesson that stuck.

❧ My Bellwether, Belle Z. ❧

Bellwether: noun: a wether or other male sheep that leads the flock, usually bearing a bell on its neck. A person or thing that assumes the leadership or forefront, as of a profession or industry. A person or thing that shows the existence or direction of a trend. —Dictionary.com

I was struggling. Clinging to the side of the only way I thought things had to be.

I was going to make my living as a musician-singer-songwriter, and that was it. It was what I loved, it was what I knew. It was how I identified myself.

It was also my rebellion. My pushback against my father and our family's business. I was determined to separate myself from the pack, not be an actor, or need my family's help professionally—especially not his. (My older, wiser, child-rearing self misses him so much these days that it's weird to remember I felt that way.)

I had veered from my solitary music pursuit a few times in my early life, heeding my dad's advice, even if I wouldn't have admitted it then. Needing to keep my union status current (health benefits made sense to me, even at that age!), in my midtwenties, I hit up my dad for "a few acting gigs." He decided that, instead of him just giving me a job as he had when I was in high school, I needed to meet some casting directors.

"Too ethnic looking," they said. (Really?)

"Not TV type." (Whatever that means.)

"You should definitely go to New York and try theater," they said. "You are just too big for the small screen." (Physically? Emotionally? WTF??)

After these bad experiences and rejections in the acting world—being told I would never work in television—my fragile identity was all the more bolstered by the attention my music brought me.

When I was twenty-eight years old, my friends Paul Gordon and Jay Gruska asked me to be in a rock musical they'd written, *Backstreet*, the one produced and financed by Johnny Starbuck. They were putting it up in a small theater in Pasadena. I had written and recorded with both these guys, and we were musically on a similar page. Unlike any other musicals I'd heard or been involved in (like my chorus girl stint in *Two Gentlemen of Verona*), their music was hip. This was at a time when musical theater had not yet crossed over into a contemporary sound, and theirs was a new approach. I loved the music.

I said yes.

Backstreet opened at the Delancey Street Theater, a converted auto garage, sometime in 1984. During its short run, my life changed.

I met Belle Zwerdling.

She knew who I was before I knew her.

She's since told me a story about coming to a party in the early eighties at my sister Jean's apartment. I sauntered in, scowling, extra cool, with my full rock 'n' roll on display. I can't remember what I wore in those days. Lots of black and shoulder pads come to mind. High-heel spiky boots. A cigarette always glued between my pouty lips.

I grunted my hellos.

She said my cool demeanor terrified and enamored her simultaneously.

She never forgot me.

In 1984 Belle had just found her calling. After years of seeking her place in the world—working as a waitress at the Rainbow Bar and Grill and the Comedy Store on the Sunset Strip—she ended up a baby partner in a theatrical agency when she joined longtime agent Bernie Carneol in his one-man operation, Progressive Artists Agency. Belle had an eye for talent and, as her new partnership required, she was on the hunt. She came to see *Backstreet* to check out our young lead, Pamela

Segall. Now known to all as Pamela Adlon, she was eighteen and had some buzz at the time.

As Belle now tells it, she loved Pammy, but I was the one who caught her attention. *Backstreet* is a musical based on the lives of a group of Venice Beach street people living, working, and loving on the boardwalk in Venice—where not long before, I'd been playing for guitar-case tips with my first love. I played Celia, the compassionate, lovelorn matriarch of the pack. And I had *killer* songs to sing.

Raw, intuitive, Belle saw something in me. That I was someone special.

That I was truly an actress.

She timidly introduced herself again.

Told me she was an agent. Asked if I had one.

I, snarling, said something like, "For what? Acting is not my bend. I'm a musician."

She came to see the show three times, eventually bringing Bernie Carneol to see if he concurred with what she was feeling in her gut.

Belle shyly made her way over to me after another performance, staring at me with something like amazement, as she tends to do, with innocence, like a child or a dog with a bone.

"*What?*" I said. "Why do you keep coming here?"

"Because I think you are amazing. If you ever decide to be an actor and want representation, let me know," she said, the words tumbling out of her mouth with such intensity, speed, and conviction, I wasn't quite sure what she had just said.

She shoved her card into my hand and ran out the door.

I kept it.

Maybe it was her enthusiasm that made me call her, or her innocence. Maybe it was my dawning maturity and the fact that the struggle for rock stardom was losing its mystique.

I'd have to go back out on the road soon to keep paying my bills, and my guilt was growing at the lack of fiscal return coming Johnny Starbuck's way. My dad had been dead since 1981. So I couldn't push back on him for buzz anymore, either.

I called Belle Z.

"Yeah, okay, you can be my agent," I said.

I think she gasped audibly on the other end of the phone.

I was her first client.

She was my first agent.

We have been together now thirty-three years—my longest relationship.

Within six months, with my newfound determination and her palpable enthusiasm to help me expand my horizons, I got the lead in a rock opera, *The Beautiful Lady*, written by Elizabeth Swados. It opened in August 1985 at the Mark Taper Forum, one of the few actual legit theaters in Los Angeles, part of the Los Angeles Music Center. I played a Russian poet named Marina Tsvetaeva during the Russian Revolution and then after the Stalin era. The piece was entirely sung and very dramatic. I won a Drama-Logue Award for my performance, and within the first month of the run was spotted by casting directors at CBS. I was asked to come read for a sitcom—a comedy—which made no sense given the unfunny nature of the performance I was giving at the time.

Shockingly, I got the gig.

The *Mary* show ran for thirteen episodes on CBS during the 1985–86 TV season, and within six months of that ending, along came *Married with Children*.

I have not stopped working since.

That thing Belle saw, that instinct in her gut, that initial reaction she had about me, has proved itself my bellwether. She predicted something would happen, and it did. I followed her lead, and things changed. She visualized my success, and it came.

She has never left my side.

She has always believed "At the end of the day, talent prevails."

And when my career has taken the inevitable dips, and I have lost sight or hope or drive or enthusiasm to wade through, she has always kept a light on. She has picked me up out of the muck, carried me through those periods when I was convinced "I'll never work again."

I've always been a bit of a tough sell as an actress; never been anyone's obvious choice. Every door had to be smashed down. And what I've had in Belle is somebody to whom the word *no* means nothing. "No" actually means "Let me call you back." The most important thing in representation is to have someone who *gets* you and will go to the mat for you, in the face of anybody saying "No" to you. That's Belle.

What I know about casting is, if you have your heart set on an apple, and an orange walks in the door, it's not that you don't like oranges, it's just that you really wanted an apple. She's always explained rejection to me in a way that it's not personal, and coming from her, I seem to always believe it. I'm much more sensitive than people realize, and by being my biggest fan and giving me unconditional love, she's been able to protect me in the most valuable ways. When I've called Belle because parts weren't coming in, she's always said, "Everybody loves you. It's just tough right now." Knowing that's what I needed to hear.

Over the years, our bond has expanded beyond our working relationship. She's celebrated with me a job well done, listened to my bullshit, fear, longing, regret, walked with me through more than her job description required. I tell her everything. I believe she tells me everything, too. She has become more to me than a business partner (though our business relationship has flourished, so her titles now include manager and production partner). She's a great friend. She is the godmother to my three children, having been present at the births of the first two, as well as my closest friend, my sister, my mother.

That beam of light of hers, I stick to very closely, as mine dims frequently, but hers never does.

Married . . . with Children

I wasn't ever supposed to be on TV.

So when I got called to audition for a new TV pilot called *Married with Children*, on an unheard-of TV network called FOX, I wasn't deeply invested in getting the gig. I was still treating acting as a way to support my *real* job: being a musician.

I'd only landed my first series regular role the previous year, on the *Mary* show, with the fantastic Mary Tyler Moore. I'd played an irreverent, chain-smoking newspaper journalist named Jo Tucker, who sat across the desk from America's girlfriend and cracked some hard jokes while blowing smoke in her face.

Terrified that the acting job wasn't secure, I continued living life as I always had. I had a band, and I kept playing gigs. Every morning, I crawled into the sunlit, daytime world of network television by way of after-hours clubs, and my own late-night shows at the Central (now the Viper Room) or Club Lingerie (now a strip club). I was a "go to bed as the sun's coming up" kind of person. My boyfriend at the time, Spyder Mittleman, a saxophone player, and I were living out a crazy, drug-fueled, bluesy, romantic love story. We were partners on the dark side. (He ultimately lost his life on that dark side; I crawled out of the hole. Grace of God!) Spyder would come to visit me on set, bleary eyed, with a black pompadour, black fingernails, and black eyeliner dripping, and I used to sneak him up to my dressing room so no one would see him. He was so clearly not TV fare, and I was trying to fit in as best as I could without having to change my ways completely.

Now that my acting gig required an early-morning call time, I struggled. I knew the opportunities were good ones. I just wasn't sure how to manage them. So I bullshitted my way through.

I took some kind of amphetamine to wake up in the morning, and then I took something to go to sleep at night. And in between, I always drank.

In hindsight, acting on *Mary* was a tipping point for me.

Trying to hold on to my identity as an up-and-coming rock star while slipping into these new TV shoes was straining. And my using and drinking escalated.

I remember someone on the show talking about sobriety on the set. I wanted to fit in and be a part of. I claimed I was sober.

I just bald-faced lied.

Years later, I credit that person as being my "Eskimo." (A term from the rooms for the person who shepherds you in.)

In spite of living in a fog, on the *Mary* show I got the laughs.

The show, not so much. *Mary* was canceled after thirteen episodes.

I really didn't know if I'd ever act again. I was back to chasing my music dream. But I'd also gotten used to the structure of what, for me, was like a nine-to-five job: working on a TV show.

I wanted to keep going. I liked it.

Luckily for me, during my TV debut on *Mary*, Ron Leavitt was cocreating *MWC*. And his wife Sharon Leavitt, who liked to call herself "the real-life Peg Bundy," had spotted me on the show. She suggested to her husband that he should check me out for the part of Peg.

That's how, in October of 1986, I got the call to audition. Two months previously, I also got the slam on the head, the incomprehensible demoralization, the bottom that woke me up, and I surrendered myself to the realization my life was unmanageable.

I had to get clean.

Newly sober from a fifteen-year (give or take) addiction to drugs and alcohol, and never before having worked or auditioned for anything without the help of some kind of happy pill or a cocktail, I was pleased-slash-terrified by the opportunity to audition.

I figured I'd have fun with it, take a chance, and add my own spin.

After reading the script, my take on Peg was that she should be kind of hot, sexy, so I got dolled up for my audition. I wore a tight dress and high heels, cat-eye glasses, and my hair piled high on my head. I'm sure it was partly my vanity. In the script, Peg was physically described as a dumpy hausfrau. Peg's audition outfit was a little closer to how I normally looked and what was in my closet. In those days I dressed slutty, eighties. I dyed my hair different colors and wore it big, with ultra-extra-hold hair-spray. I also, like Peg was described in the script, chain-smoked. The pilot episode of *MWC* was "a down-on-his-luck shoe sales-man tries to decide whether to go to a basketball game or meet his new neighbors with his *lazy* wife, Peg." The characters tore each other apart from page one, and slung mud at each other con-stantly, but they had been married for sixteen years, and, between the lines, it was clear they were bonded. By love? Yeah, maybe. But by habit and commitment, for sure.

The working title was *This Is Not the Cosby Show.* It was a bit-ter, nasty, seriously funny look into the lives of a shoe salesman, his high-school-sweetheart-turned-wife, and their two kids. It was dark and rude and read like nothing else I'd ever seen on television. That removed some of the jitters, as I figured no one would ever take it seriously, so what was there to be nervous about? I loved the script, but given my dark sensibilities, I figured few others would.

Peg was described as a slovenly couch potato (a la Roseanne Barr, a successful stand-up comedian at the time) who sat around the house eating bonbons and constantly complaining and giving her husband a hard time. Just a total pain in his ass. The breakdown of her character was not at all flattering. Al Bundy was originally sup-posed to be a Sam Kinison type who screamed all of the time. But I felt there had to be something more between this married couple than hostile bantering. Something that allowed them to tear into each other with such verve. Something that held them together: great sex.

I decided that even if Al and Peg weren't having sex very fre-quently (this was a constant theme of *Married with Children*, that a married man no longer wants to fuck his wife, and a lot of people related to the sentiment), they still had the kind of chemistry that meant a seriously hot sex life, even if it was now only a memory, and one that Peg longed for, making her beg for sex constantly.

Anyhow, I showed up for my audition at an office on the Sunset Gower Studios lot, high heels clacking, and walked into what I guessed was an executive's office. Really, it looked more like a dorm room. I was met by Michael Moye and Ron Leavitt, not your typical television producers, who looked like real-life Al Bundys in a room strewn with papers, books, and literally, garbage: pizza boxes, soda cans, cigarette butts, half-eaten lunches.

Throwing newspapers off the couch so I could grab a corner seat, they filled me in on how the show had come about. They'd been approached by Columbia/TriStar, where they'd both had successful shows before (*The Jeffersons*, *Silver Spoons*) to develop a show for a new network that was trying to push the envelope. They'd been mandated to write irreverently, and they sure did.

They dug my sexed-up approach to Peg. I made it through the first round of auditions and was asked to come back to read with their three choices for Al Bundy. There were two other female actors, including Rita Wilson, and two other male actors whom I don't remember at all. I remember no one but Ed O'Neill. Ed and I had it going on from the moment we met. He was a big, sexy, everyman kind of guy, and we had instant chemistry. Other than keeping a straight face (a constant challenge for the next eleven years with this seriously funny guy), being with Ed was a breeze.

Ed never felt like an actor to me. Or at least not the self-absorbed, self-involved type of actors I had met before then. I think Ed liked me, too, because I'm not very actory either. I brought a little bit of street to the role, and he responded to that. We got along instantly, and we were very funny with each other. We were hired together.

The original child actors playing Kelly and Bud were not Christina Applegate and David Faustino, but after we filmed the pilot, it was decided the kids they'd first cast weren't a good fit, and both parts were recast. As soon as Chrissie and Dave were brought in, they made us "the Bundys." Ed, Christina, David, and me, from the very moment the kids joined the show, ended up being "the ensemble." Chemistry is impossible to define. Cannot be taught or manipulated. It just is or it isn't. We had it.

Christina was young and blonde and beautiful, and she was also a pro, since she'd been taken along to auditions by her actress mother and had made her acting debut in a commercial at five months. She'd already appeared on several TV shows by this point. David had started acting even younger, at *three* months, playing Lily Tomlin's *daughter* on one of her TV specials. They were both so talented.

Ironically, we were all pretty mean spirited, even offscreen. In a loving way, sure, but the jokes were how we related. I definitely think there's a reason we were all drawn to that show. All four of us had some Bundy in us.

So here I was.

With an awesome job.

Coupled with a deep-down belief that I would be found out for the fraud I knew I was—having worked very little as an actor, and with a minimal amount of "training"—I stood frozen in my sober shoes. Afraid to rock any boats or ask too many questions; just kind of holding my breath so nobody would see how terrified I was. The last thing I wanted to do was show up late, or not at all, or mess up my lines, or any number of things that even one night of vodka and blow could lead me to do. I did not want to fuck up in the face of so many strangers, and—though I'd always been able to show up on a job even when using—this time felt different. Like if I went down that road again, there really would be no coming back, I really would be down too far to return. I clung to my sobriety.

Looking back to how I'd gotten here, I felt lucky to be standing at all. My lifelong music aspirations were a constant merry-go-round of near misses. From an early age, I'd been told my music was special, that I could really sing, that my dreams were not just pie in the sky, they were what I could count on, any day now, bound to happen, not just rhetoric.

I was told I was a "star" even before I could drive a car.

I believed "them."

And put all my eggs in that basket.

Yeah, and nothing happened.

I was stuck, bitter, and disappointed by the time I was twenty-seven. Uncomfortable with those feelings, I did what I'd come to do: numb them with my growing dependence on drugs and alcohol.

After my part in the musical *Backstreet*, the doors had started swinging open, and I walked through them all, sort of the same way I'd walked through most major changes in my life, both the good ones and the bad ones: numb and detached.

I *think* I was excited?

Having grown up where I was now employed, it all felt familiar. Yet because of my lack of real experience and my years of detachment from being where I was, it felt like it was happening to someone else or that any day they would realize I didn't know what the fuck I was doing and bring in my replacement.

Thank God I was simultaneously learning the principles of living one day at a time. I could face anything in small increments. I could do anything until I went to bed at night. Sometimes the thought of going to work the next day was the same struggle I had of not picking up a drink or a drug.

Because I was afraid. Of everything.

New sobriety.

An anxious state.

People felt unsafe.

Intimacy confusing.

Drugs and alcohol had given me the illusion of connection. The false camaraderie of booze and pills had been as far as I could get with other folks. So it all made me squirm: Forcing connections with my costars and the crew. Having all eyes on me. And doing it sober. This was new. It is said that the alcoholic hears things a little louder, lights shine a bit brighter, like an emotional amplifier. With alcohol, the alcoholic is just trying to turn things down.

Now I had no way of doing that.

I'd have to tell myself "If you don't want to go to work tomorrow, you don't have to go." Same way I told myself "If

you really want to get high tomorrow, you can, just not today."
I always felt different in the morning. That didn't stop me from
feeling that way again the next night. But still, I stayed sober, and
I kept showing up for work.

We had a great response to our show from the beginning.

On a small scale.

When we debuted in the spring of 1987, it was hard to find
the FOX network on the TV dial, so our success was based on the
week-to-week studio audience response.

Which was uproarious. We got enormous laughs. It felt awesome. The rush of people laughing and the rhythm of knowing
when to hold for the joke felt natural and exhilarating. And the
sitcom medium, with its live audience, felt more and more like a
place I remembered being: on the stage, be it in *Two Gentlemen of
Verona* or singing in a band.

Our very odd, very irreverent, dark comedy was hitting a
chord, and because it was a new network, with just a small amount
of programming, we were given the airtime (they'd air us three
times a night and then all throughout the week!) and the creative
time to grow and catch on.

In hindsight, it was a luxury. Doesn't happen these days.

Shows are on and off after a few weeks if the ratings are not
substantial out of the gate. Streaming sites upload entire seasons
overnight and then, when they don't perform as expected, drop
them just as quickly.

That was not our journey. We had time.

Once I started getting shows under my belt and the affirmation of laughter, I was able to be more comfortable in that role. And then, familiarly, it was sort of like playing in a band. You rely on those people around you, that troupe of actors, and eventually you're able to experiment, try things, take chances. So the more I did it, the less afraid I was. I think being a musician helped. Comedy is so much about time and rhythm. And if it's well written, which that show was, then the rhythm is clear.

Every year on a TV show might be your last. Every year, the bean counters weigh in, one way or the other: In the red. In the black. Here today. Seriously gone tomorrow, more times than not. But, *MWC*, we kept getting picked up again and again. I kept knowing I'd have a job after the summer. For a serial freelancer who'd always worked gig to gig, mostly as a musician, now as an actor, this was a deep breath.

As each season went by, I became more and more aware of just what a special situation *Married with Children* was. In show business, it is the rarest of exceptions when you can consider yourself employed for any extended period of time. I knew this from birth, having grown up watching my dad hustle for jobs, wait for ratings, be in development, hope the network would buy the pitch, get cancelled, be renewed, sell the movie, shoot the movie—one job to the next, always lining up the next job before the present one was done. Never sure there would *be* a next job. Having dreams shattered, getting up anyway, doing it over and over.

After the third season of *MWC*, in 1989, we were renewed for two years in a row. This was unheard of—an almost unknown occurrence. It was also a sign of great success and a vote of confidence that our show would reach that great nirvana: *syndication*! The goal of every four-camera situation comedy was to make it past that third year, which would then guarantee a hundred produced episodes and syndication, which is where the real "job security" is.

But this was back then, and there we were. At the doors of nirvana.

I was aware of the plateau, but my newfound sobriety had me so tethered to the "one day at a time" of it all that I didn't much pay attention to what was going on beyond each day. Actually the whole experience had a hazy, dreamlike quality. It just didn't seem to actually be happening to me. I could process it only in small doses. One day led into the next, and the next, and then, suddenly, I was famous.

Midway through our second year, they sent Ed and me on a promotional tour to the middle of the country. The Mall of America or something like it. At that point, nobody really knew about the FOX network, and so we were sure nobody knew about us, either. We were scheduled to do this kind of rinky-dink little parade, with me dressed as Peg and Ed as Al and both of us on this little float. We weren't expecting anything at all. But there were actually people lined up and cheering. We were shocked. It was interesting that people knew who we were, but it also made me deeply uncomfortable. My first brush with fame was for acting, a profession I still wasn't sure about. I couldn't quite wrap my head around it, and so, because I was dressed as this character, Peg, I told myself that *she* was famous, not me.

I always really wanted Peg to look different from me, so I could continue to play music and keep separation between my two worlds. And that costume actually served me. Even at the height of *MWC*'s popularity, when I was out of "Peg drag," I could walk around completely anonymously. At a certain point, Ed couldn't go out without being recognized, which used to drive him crazy. At the height of our popularity, when we'd go on press junkets, people would scream, "Yo, Al!" He hated it. "I felt like I was Porky Pig," he'd always say.

We had to have security guards escort each of us home from the show tapings.

We all got crazy fan mail.

Irreverent requests for everything from Peg's shoes to her bra (once stolen from the Frederick's of Hollywood Lingerie Museum and Celebrity Lingerie Hall of Fame, on Hollywood Boulevard).

I had this one guy so obsessed with Peg that he thought she was his mom and, simultaneously, his girlfriend. And he didn't really like his mom *or* his girlfriend. He wrote scary letters. It was insane. He had to be tracked down and stopped.

The success was incredible; impossible to believe, almost. We were a show no other network would have considered, airing on a network that barely existed, telling the raunchiest tale of a loser family held together by history and insults. Funny, for sure. But since from the start you could barely find the FOX network on your dial (rabbit ears helped, which we even made jokes about on *MWC*!), success was a long shot. The longest shot. The highest hurdle.

And then there was the fact that I was even in that boat. After I'd been swimming/drowning, year after year after year. With all that attention, it was even harder than usual for me to stay in my body. To accept what was going on around me. With me.

Feeling connected to anything had always been my struggle. Making commitments, following through. All of that had always been incredibly tough. Years of staying fucked up can do that to a girl.

Here I was, committed, with a seven-year contract. Seeing the same folks day after day, having people depend on me—all things I'd been able to kind of skate around having to do for most of my adult life during my very extended adolescence.

During my eleven years on our show, I grew up, surrounded and protected by *Married with Children*. I felt loved and supported by my extended family.

After the painful loss of a late-term pregnancy, I got pregnant with Sarah in 1993 and then again with Jackson in 1995. And both times, my amazing executive producers insisted that I go home for the duration, doing their part to ensure safe, successful arrivals.

They made sure I never lost a paycheck:

I was Peg on the phone from her mother's.

I was Peg on the phone while on a road trip.

I was Peg on the phone from Disney World.

And then, as each baby was born, they'd set up a nursery for me next to my dressing room, so my babies were always with me.

They were just amazing.

* * *

For the 1996–97 season, our eleventh, FOX moved our time slot to Saturday nights, and the ratings dipped. We weren't really surprised. Every year, we'd thought, *Wow, we're still here.* Especially after we'd survived Terry Rakolta, who'd tried to have us taken off the air during our third season because she was upset that her kids were watching something she deemed so vulgar.

Rakolta was a mother and a homemaker from Bloomfield Hills, Michigan. She objected to the content of an episode, "Her Cups Runneth Over," which aired on January 15, 1989, in which Al and his friend Steve Rhoades (played by David Garrison) go to a department store to buy a bra for Peg and see a naked model—from the back.

She complained in writing to *MWC*'s sponsors, several of which, including McDonald's and Procter & Gamble, stopped advertising on the show. FOX bowed to the pressure somewhat by moving the sitcom back from 8:30 p.m. to 9:00 p.m. It also shelved an upcoming episode about Peg, Kelly, and Marcy all getting their periods at the same time on a camping trip—worried that could be found offensive.

However, by the following year, most of the sponsors had returned to the fold, and *MWC*'s ratings had risen, something that some observers (and even Terry Rakolta herself) attribute partly to her attempted boycott. The controversy landed us in the *New York Times*, and we sent Mrs. Rakolta flowers every year, which I'm sure pissed her off to no end.

I was so proud not to cower in the face of a demand for censorship. My response to the haters was and is always: "If you don't like it, change the channel."

By the last two seasons, however, it had started to feel like we were telling the same jokes over and over. We kept asking everybody at the network, "Is this it? Are we done?" They would never say either way, so the writers never wrote a last episode. We all kind of left one another for that hiatus after our eleventh season thinking we'd be back.

And then, in the spring of 1997, they pulled it.

Ed was walking out of a convenience store in Ohio when he received the news. I was at home, cleaning up Sarah's room, when the phone rang.

Are you fucking kidding me? I thought. *That's it?*

It had been in the ether that we might not come back, and they'd purposefully written the conclusion of the previous season to be open-ended. But we were the network's flagship show, and we never thought we wouldn't get a final episode, at least.

Peter Roth, then the head of FOX and now the chief content officer of Warner Bros. Television, was so mortified that he had to be the one to cancel the show. He took the time to personally apologize to me over lunch, which I always appreciated.

All of us who were involved with *Married with Children* were pissed off and disappointed by how it ended. But, with time, the shock wore off. We all got to a place of acceptance. It's almost fitting. Of course that's how the never-a-happy-ending Bundys would end: unceremoniously, just dropped off a cliff.

I'd always wanted kids. I never had any doubt in my mind that I'd be a mom. I remember hearing my clock hammering with each passing year. I'd had conversations with myself, confirming that I would parent alone if the right daddy didn't show up. Finally having steady employment made all of that even more possible. But still, a partner would be the better way to go.

At first, I wasn't sure Jack was the right one to get that serious with.

Baby kind of serious.

Or maybe he was. I just didn't know it yet.

Not sure that we were much more than a three-month fling, I was conflicted about the pregnancy. Jack and I were just getting to know each other. It seemed too soon to make anything permanent. Yet we had done the most permanent of all things. We had conceived.

I wanted the baby; I just wasn't sure about us. We barely had time to have those "us" conversations, as I miscarried at eight weeks. I hadn't told many people I was pregnant. (I'm half Jewish, and my superstitious half-Jewish side knew not to tell.)

So no one knew, no harm, no foul. My bosses at *MWC* might have suspected, but they didn't let on.

Jack and I stayed together. Decided we would keep getting to know each other. And things were good. We tried to not be sloppy about our contraception. Thought we were safe. But then, three months after that first loss, we were pregnant again. This time we were committed. I was absolutely elated.

I was a little nervous, but I told my bosses on the show. I didn't know how they would deal with my pregnancy. My super-

Ruby

My years of childbearing and child rearing have been fraught wit[
extremes—beginning with the sudden disappearance of my ghos[
child; my children's older sister. Before Sarah, there was Ruby. Ruby,
who made front-page tabloid news without ever taking a breath.

Married with Children was into its fourth season and going
strong. While on the show, I met drummer Jack White in 1991, a
rock star in his own right, thanks to his years with Ike and Tina
Turner, Redbone, and Rick Springfield.

Within three months of dating, I was pregnant.

In my first five years of sobriety, I'd had a few short-lived
dating situations, but nothing serious. New sobriety. New gig.
I wasn't exactly looking for a new relationship. After the mis-
steps of my youth, I incorporated vigilant birth control into my
occasional dating. But I'd had a few sloppy nights with Jack, and
boom! Knocked up.

menschy bosses, coproducers Ron Leavitt and Michael Moye, were just great. As usual, they thought of me first, in the same kind and loving way they always considered the lives of their employees before the job. (Amazing guys, those two.) They decided it made perfect sense that Peg might get pregnant and asked if I would be okay with them writing my pregnancy into the show. I thought that was a fantastic idea. So when the Bundys returned for season five, Peggy was with child.

Of course, Al's character was annoyed: oh God, another mouth to feed. And the writers got maximum comedy out of the situation, writing it that Al couldn't remember even having sex with Peg, because he'd gotten drunk and passed out, and she'd taken advantage of him. Classic *Married with Children*.

My pregnancy was a healthy one, nothing abnormal. At five months, I had a routine amniocentesis, the test that was suggested you have if you were over thirty-five in order to check the health and find out the sex of the baby.

She was fine.

All good news.

At seven months, my pregnancy took a turn. I went for my checkup, and I'd lost all of my amniotic fluid. For no apparent reason.

I didn't feel anything, so I hadn't been able to tell I'd lost my fluid. The baby was okay, but my doctor told me I had to be hospitalized, confined to my bed, in hopes that the fluid would return. Maybe I'd been overdoing it at work? No one could pinpoint what had happened or why. I was just told to stay still and calm, calm being the hardest part—but I did. I lived with a heart monitor strapped to my belly in a hospital room and literally got up only to piss.

Her heart beat on.

My fluid never returned.

But her heart beat on . . .

While I was in the hospital, the writers wrote that Peg was visiting family out of town. I could just record some lines for Peg to deliver over the phone, stay on bed rest, and focus on taking care of us. Ever generous, they came to the hospital, and I recorded dialogue from my bed.

After about ten days in the hospital, the fluid still hadn't come back, but they told me I could go home, as long as I stayed on bed rest. My doctor gave me a monitor to check her heartbeat.

The next weekend, at seven and a half months, I went to the doctor for a routine checkup, and everything was fine. But that afternoon, I couldn't find her beats on my home monitor. Belle came to get me and rushed my anxious self back to Cedars-Sinai for a closer look. They found Ruby. All good: she'd been hiding.

But by five o'clock that afternoon, back at home, I couldn't find her heartbeats again! I was flipping out. I figured she must be hiding, but I couldn't find her. I was eating to wake her up, rubbing, and prodding, and rolling into different positions to find the sweet spot where her lovely heart was beating.

Nothing.

By this time, I was fully bonded with her. After many months of a lot of concentrated time, focusing, praying, checking, and double-checking the little one inside me, I could just tell something was wrong.

I called my doctor.

"I can't find her heartbeat again," I said.

"Get in the car and come back here, come back to Cedars," he said, his voice betraying that he too could intuit something was wrong.

Jack drove us through the crowded Saturday night Hollywood traffic, and it was a miracle we didn't mow down anybody. *Nobody* was driving fast enough. The gridlock was insurmountable. Yet we tried to remain calm.

By the time we got to the hospital, though, I just knew.

My sweet doctor, Uzzi Reiss, was already there, waiting for us. His face did not look hopeful. He knew Ruby pretty well by this point, too. And when you are a baby doctor, I think you have a sense of how things are.

When he examined me, he told me that her heart had stopped.

He wasn't surprised. I guess because she'd been in distress for so long.

I was surprised. And I wasn't.

It felt like my heart had stopped too.

I was lying on the exam table, with her little body inside of me. Not sure when she had actually left, but knowing she was gone.

I spent the next thirty-two hours trying to push out my dead daughter in hopes of having a natural delivery.

Delirious from the Pitocin-induced labor, and the Valium— or whatever the fuck they were giving me—I was finally sliced open, and her little three-pound body was taken from me for autopsy.

She had a full head of black hair.

And she was beautiful.

I think in my hysterical, delirious state of mind, I was expecting her to look shriveled and distorted—maybe charred. All such weird thoughts.

But she looked fine. She had all her parts.

I spent the next year *knowing* it was my fault.

(It wasn't.)

So, then, what had happened?

"Without a medical reason," is what they said.

"Act of God," is what they call 60 percent of stillbirths.

Born. Yet still.

Kind of a gentle image for such a tragedy. The birth process is so active, to have at the end of so much activity a quiet and still young soul.

Not satisfied that the explanation "act of God" on Ruby's death certificate was actually reason enough, I went to various doctors, probably once a month, for almost a year. Convinced something must be wrong with me, I thought for sure I was mysteriously stricken with some grave illness that they just hadn't found, and that's what had taken her from me. Maybe I had a bad heart like my mom. Maybe I had cancer again. Maybe I had AIDS. I couldn't wrap my brain around the possibility that I hadn't done something wrong to cause her death. I knew bad things happened randomly. But I needed more of an explanation. There was none.

I went to a support group. I did a lot of reading about still-births. I prayed and went to meetings and eventually shared my darkest thoughts and fears, and with disclosure, they slowly started to dissipate.

Six weeks after losing Ruby, I returned to work. But that was all I could do.

They dealt with Peg losing her baby as if it had all been a dream. That she'd never been pregnant. It was just Al's "scary dream." The perfect way to handle it, given the irreverent nature of our show. Of course, just because Peg was never seen losing the baby didn't mean my stillbirth wasn't public knowledge. It was everywhere in the press. Odd to go through something so personal in public. Paparazzi were a bit more respectful in 1992, but they were still lurking. Looking for dirt. Hoping for an unflattering pic.

I went to the set five days a week, and then I came right back home. Afraid to be of the world. At the market. At the mall. Didn't want you to see me. Not because I was fucking famous and her death had become news worldwide, but because I was afraid you would really see me.

My broken parts.

And even I couldn't stand to "see me."

So why would you?

Ashamed, I hid.

I obsessed. Looking for answers. I knew I must be responsible. That I'd fucked up somehow.

Maybe she died because I wasn't sure I was in love with her dad at that early stage of our relationship.

Maybe she died because I didn't "take it easy."

Maybe she died because I wasn't going to be a good mom, and God knew that and took her away.

Maybe she didn't like me.

Like I was cursed or something.

I was nuts.

Ego wouldn't let up. It had to be my fault. I'd done something horrible to my child. I was sure of it.

It took me a whole year to find a place to put her passing. Finally, something made sense. After numerous visits to shrinks and healers, stillbirth support groups, psychics. All in the pursuit of answers.

Where did Ruby go?

Why did she die?

If there really was "no medical reason" . . . what the fuck happened?

My answer came in Buddhist teachings. I don't remember which road led me to them. But this is what was explained to me, from a Buddhist perspective. I'm paraphrasing. I'm not a Buddhist, but this made sense:

Her purpose had been fulfilled in the short time she was here.

Which meant I'd have to believe she was here for a "purpose."

That we all are.

I believe that.

I don't know that we always know what that purpose is, but I do believe we all have a destiny to be fulfilled.

So, Buddhisty-speaking, it was explained to me that powerful souls come in and out of this life quickly, because their work here is done. They have passed on the lesson they were meant to pass on. Nothing left for them to do. So Ruby completed her mission. With that concept in mind, I asked different questions. I had a shift in perception.

Ruby was fierce. She did so much in her short stay.

She gave me greater understanding and appreciation for life in general, not to mention the whole childbirth thing. What a fucking miracle that is! That any of us makes it through. She brought her dad and me closer, and I did fall more in love with him.

The lessons I learned by having my heart broken so deeply were exactly, and perfectly, the lessons I needed to learn. And they were, just so, the time and place for me to learn them. My heart broke, and I didn't fucking die.

It passed.

The school bell rang.

I could breathe again.

Ruby taught me that lesson by leaving so quickly.

She taught me I could hold more than I'd ever imagined I could. Her loss had let me revisit all that I had lost before her. My mom, my dad, my young self that I had trashed with drugs and alcohol. They all showed up. Unfinished, undone.

I grieved.

All of them.

All of those sudden passings that I had stuffed away.

She let me feel my strength.

She confirmed my faith in something greater than myself. That God of mine got redefined, and my partnership renewed. I really thought losing her was God's punishment. Which meant I believed in a punishing God. Which really sucked and, actually, felt more like a mad dad than like a God that wants me to be happy, joyous, and free.

I took a look at all of that. I changed what I believed.

My God, or universal consciousness, as I call it, doesn't punish or pass judgment. It's a source of comfort in my human condition. Walks by my side. Did not kill Ruby to punish me.

I did not kill Ruby.

Ruby was done. Her highest purpose—some of which I can name, most of which I'll never know—was fulfilled. There would be no Sarah, no Jackson, no Esmé without Ruby, and I am grateful for her short visit because of that.

I eventually looked at the whole awful situation as something I would share with others someday, which is sort of how I look at everything. I don't handle life's inconsistencies very well. I scare easily and don't do well with surprises.

But if I can share the fear with you, it takes the focus off me.

And then I'm not so scared.

It's service.

Sarah, Strong and Tall

Tomorrow the movers are coming to put Sarah's bed in storage. Her piano will be moved to our house in Idaho. I stripped her bed and packed away her blankets and comforter. I kept walking in and out of there. And then stood frozen in the middle of the room. Her stuffed animals and books are mostly in boxes. All but a few. There's dirty old Rags, a white dog with brown spots. I left him on her bookshelf. I've kept all her clothes in the closet because I can't bear to take them out. They are her clothes. They smell like her.

She's not dead.

She has left for college, and we need the space. I've been afraid to change her room because I'm afraid she'll never come back if I do. I'm afraid she will forget me and home and us. I'm afraid she'll turn into me at her age. I tried so hard to make sure that never happened. That she didn't have the mother I'd had.

That she didn't become the daughter I'd been. I told myself it would be different when I had kids.

That they wouldn't be afraid of me.

That I would listen to them.

That they would never rush to leave home.

That I wouldn't die on them.

So far, so good.

Sarah is my first. My first that made it, I mean. After Ruby, I was a nervous wreck carrying Sarah. So terrified I would fail her somehow, still not wholeheartedly grasping the idea that 60 percent of stillbirths, like Ruby, have "no medical reason." The belief that I must have done something wrong still hanging around—faintly, but there nonetheless.

Sarah is my brave do-over. I was so afraid to do it again, even to try again, but I'd reached the point of no return. If I were to give baby making another go, at age thirty-nine, I needed to act fast. I got pregnant quickly. Actually, on my wedding night to Jack, November 27, 1993. Another of my crazy superstitions was that maybe Ruby, my ghost child, hadn't made it because of my not being married to her dad at the time. Ruby had come to us so quickly, we still weren't 100 percent sure about each other. Maybe, somehow, she knew that the union was not yet certain.

But by the time we conceived Sarah, we were on solid ground.

I was going to give this kid every possible shot.

Fingers and toes crossed.

All papers in order.

Wedding bands in place.

Checking her monthly, making sure her beats were strong. By the seventh month, my paranoia that she might disappear like Ruby had made me go to my doctor's office weekly; I felt restless and uneasy until I could see and hear her steady heartbeats on the heart monitor. By my final month, I needed to visit my doctor daily, just to check. And have him confirm that what I was hearing was her heart beating.

My final two weeks, my doctor admitted me to the hospital so that my baby and I could rest and wait for her due date. I slept contentedly, surrounded by the hospital staff, waiting for her lungs to mature, her heart hooked up to a monitor. *Thump-thump, thump-thump.* Sarah emerged safely via C-section, on August 7, 1994.

I felt victorious.

Elated.

In love.

Ruby has never been forgotten. But like a balloon, the loss of her drifted into the clouds, and Sarah's arms wrapped around the place she'd left behind. When Sarah came, she gave tangible purpose to the loss of Ruby.

Sarah was my "starter kid." My most special firstborn. I was cautious, clingy, anxious. Nobody knows how to be a mom. She unavoidably took on some of my first-time-mom anxiety, as most number ones do—with maybe an extra dose, considering the nine months of terror I'd surrounded her with while in utero.

When Sarah was nine months old, we got pregnant again. Jack and I were definitely brought together for this higher purpose. We never had to try. We just got pregnant. Even while breast-feeding, which they say isn't supposed to happen.

Just as I had finally started to loosen my grip a bit on my sweet Sarah, stopped breast-feeding, gotten my mommy legs, and become confident she wouldn't break if I left her side. (Most days, I brought her with me to the set of *Married with Children*.) Now I felt a need to hold her even closer, knowing this would be my only time with just her.

Sarah found her "security blankets." She had her little stuffed dog Rags always by her side and also a collection of other friendly stuffed creatures—at least thirty—surrounding her at bedtime, to watch her sleep, keep her safe. Our nightly ritual. Setting them all up. Laboriously making sure all eyes were on her.

I remember her tears, at age six, on the day I insisted we give Rags a bath. Her little body, shaking and sobbing, as I reassured her that he'd be okay if we stuck him in the washing machine. That he would still be Rags. So convinced that he'd be washed away, that something bad would happen, she won. In all his twenty years, Rags has landed in soap and water only once. And it wasn't that day. It was a day when it just wasn't that big a deal anymore.

Because that's how it is with kids. All the big deals end up not so, eventually.

You just gotta wait 'em out.

Before Rags, she had Geraldine the Beanie Baby Giraffe that I kept triples of stashed in a hall closet after that first time we misplaced her, and Sarah panicked and crumbled. From then on, the few times Geraldine was misplaced, I'd slyly slip a new Geraldine into Sarah's backpack or the collection by the side of her bed.

Through her elementary school years, I called her Sarah, Shy and Tall. She was always the tallest one in her class, and self-conscious about it. I loved her stature and thought nothing of her puppylike clumsiness—just figured she'd need some time to figure out what went where; to grow into her body—but she was never comfortable with how it made her stand out. With all that height, and those long limbs, I figured she was a budding supermodel.

Sarah was shy as a kid. She was never the kid to make the first move with other kids. Waited to be asked for a playdate, rather than instigate. Fine with me. (I always hated playdates.)

She is neither pushy nor overbearing, and never was. What I see in her now, is—probably what it was all along—she has a way of letting things unfold, not forcing situations. She has instinctively always known the right time, the respectful approach.

Sarah has that most appealing quality of being the pretty girl that doesn't know she is.

Doesn't need to flaunt or prove.

She wears herself well, even her height.

Now a beautiful five foot eleven inches.

Like I said, I was not very fond of playdates. I really had to struggle to hang out with other moms. Not that they were bad moms. Not at all. I was awkward with strangers, as I'd always been. By the time Sarah was five, my marriage to Jack was in a precarious place. As we tried to sort through what ultimately ended up in the demise of our union, I was trying to keep it under wraps, trying to protect my kids, and my husband, and I didn't know how to keep my emotions in check. Plus, small talk, a requirement of playdates, is not my strong suit.

There was also that "celebrity thing." Sometimes you don't know if other people are hanging out with you because they like you and your kids, or because they're somewhat enamored of you. As a famous person, you have extra radar for that shit. And I wanted to be only with families whose kids really liked my kids, not anyone who hoped that the fairy dust of celebrity would rub off on them. Unfortunately, a few intrusive interactions on the playground were a good excuse to distance myself from everyone before really giving anyone a chance. Maybe Sarah's "shyness" was more about my own social anxiety, which, of course, showed up in my parenting.

Sadly, my marriage to Jack ended when Sarah was six. Sarah, her little brother, Jackson, and I, kept to ourselves a lot during that time of turmoil. It echoed how I'd grown up. It was what I knew to do. Secrets are secrets, whether they're rooted in the kind of tumultuous things my family of origin had tried to hide from the outside world, or the ways that a celebrity has to shield her private life. So being our own unit was comfortable for me. We mostly stayed at home as a family—preferred it that way, really.

We always did, and continue to, enjoy one another's company.

As a result, Sarah may not have received the greatest of social skills until she could figure them out on her own. Not from her solitary mother.

We take the good with the bad.

She was never one for sports or dance classes. We tried them all. She did, however, like the small kids' theater groups we found for her. She started being in after-school productions at ten years old, and my quiet, shy, tall girl started to bloom.

I introduced her to music. I had given her piano lessons from the time she was four. I hoped she'd take to it and never forced it on her. Knowing that she came from a musical gene pool, I'd crossed my fingers it would pass down. I never made her practice, just provided the space and instruction if she wanted it. Slowly, on her own, it started to take hold. Sarah started to love it. She showed she was a natural musician. That thing you can't teach, she had. And in some ways, I believe music did for her what it had done for me.

Gave her a place.

A vocabulary.

A way to communicate, to engage.

When my family gets together on holidays, everybody plays music. All of the cousins. My brother David's oldest boy, Bo, would always get up and perform right away. Sarah was the last one to join in. She was timid. Her younger brother, Jackson, also a natural musician, was not, and he always got out there before her. She stepped forward eventually, usually performing something she wrote herself, always proving the adage "Save the best for last."

She is the most instinctive, natural musician in my family.

Junior year of high school, college tours, SAT, applications, and—there she goes!

She's gone.

It all happened so fast.

Twelve years of school wasn't enough time.

I was just gearing up.

Just understanding how to be her mother. Like a dog chasing its tail, round and round, I never felt I caught up. I still needed to rub off on her. I still had info to upload. And because of my own experience, leaving home and not looking back, my DNA thought I'd never have another chance.

When I was sixteen, I pretty much lived in my '66 Nova. By seventeen, I was strung out on diet pills and Red Mountain wine. I'd had several boyfriends, sex, an abortion, and was moving into my first apartment on my own—no roommate. I left home and never came back.

I couldn't wait to move out of my family house.

The one I tiptoed through. The one I whispered in.

I made sure it was different for Sarah. And it was.

Still, my input was no longer the first voice she heard. As it should be. I was on the list. But the list was long now, with friends and mentors.

I was afraid I was at the end of the line.

My daughter loves me. No doubt.

My friends say I've done a good job raising her, because she is not a clingy, needy, call-your-mom-four-times-a-day type.

Sucks.

I did too good of a job. How did that happen?

She needed the autonomy of going east for college. Away from LA, far enough away to hear her own voice. I get it. We are a strong, opinionated family. An identity of one's own can require distance. She knew to take it.

She went to a private liberal arts school, Kenyon College, which is in the middle of Ohio. The middle of nowhere Ohio: a little town called Gambier. Considered the most beautiful campus in the United States, Kenyon College was a trek from Los Angeles. When she and I landed in Columbus, we didn't know our way to the school. It was nighttime, country roads with few streetlights to show the way. We drove through the wilderness. We were both anxious. She, about her first college days, and me, absolutely terrified about dropping her off. We got the GPS wrong, couldn't get our directions right.

She started crying.

I started crying.

"I just think I want to go home." She broke down. "I'm not ready for this. I don't know where I *am*!"

"Okay, let's go," I said.

I whipped the car around to head back to the airport. (Way to go, Mom. Not an encouraging word, just an escape hatch.)

"Why are we here? Why did you pick this school?" I screamed at her. "It's too far from home. What if you get sick, what if you get hurt? What am I going to do without you??"

I broke, right along with her.

That dark night, pulled over on the side of the road, surrounded by cornfields, lit by a thousand stars, my sweet Sarah and I traded places back and forth. Me, the child. She, the adult. Me, the adult. She, my child.

Back and forth until our fear soothed into hysterical laughter, and the reassurance that our reactions were "all quite normal" when the first kid goes to college.

We made our way to the Holiday Inn Express, where we shared a room with two twin beds, hoping to sleep before the next morning's check-in at school. I was able to stay in my parental hammock, calming her fears, letting her voice them without my reacting.

As soon as I left her at college, it began.

I missed my daughter.

The oldest of my three children.

The one who broke me in and taught me love like I never knew.

The one who paved the way for the other two, because I couldn't believe how amazing loving her was. I had to do it one more time—and one more time after that.

I miss her because she is away now. Off to college, home for a week. Off for the summer, home for two . . .

I miss her because I really wasn't ready to let her go.

And I wondered about her as she embarked on her college life. Is she still kind of nervous in new situations? Will she find "her people"? So many fears I had for my daughter. Not that I dared to tell her. Didn't want to be that kind of mother.

Instead, I've observed.

And trusted.

And I feel happy with what I see.

Four years later. Sarah, now twenty-one. And really ready to launch. Visiting her at Kenyon College, I watch my daughter out the coffee shop window. A brisk Ohio afternoon in January, under a rare blue sky. Maybe the sky followed us here from California. I sip my cappuccino and peer stealthily over the pages of my book so she can't see me stare.

Not wanting to intrude on the reunion she's having with friends: a litter of puppies, nuzzling, necking, tumbling, all happening on the steps of Wiggin Street Coffee.

I participate from afar, in awe of the joy and appreciation, love and camaraderie. I beam at her. The tangle of arms and legs, hugging and kissing, squealing at the arrival of alumni. It's the afternoon before her senior thesis: sharing the stage in a two-woman play written by playwright and TV writer Sarah Treem. My theater major has completed the program. Friends and family have come from all around to share with her.

To celebrate her.

To love her.

As is the case in all relationships—marriage, business, children (maybe even more so with children)—the key to maintaining the bond is staying current. Observant and open to "who we are now." Children move so quickly. And they grow so dramatically.

I marvel at how just when I think, "*This* is how I do it," my kids change.

When Sarah was eight, she had a period where she talked and talked all the time. Driving to the Westside from the 818 area code to Creative Kids Youth Theater, she yammered nonstop.

Just when I understood that all I needed to do was listen, without the radio on, she fell silent on those long car rides to and from after-school activities. She entered her pensive period, and I had to be quiet too.

And now, with Sarah, the transformation is most palpable as

she graduates college. "Who she is now" feels very much as if I'm meeting her for the first time. So much has happened for her over these past four years.

And I like her.

Always love her.

As we walk to dinner at the Village Inn, I watch her with her friends. This is the Sarah I'm delighted to meet, although I'm somewhat stunned by how she's grown. I have watched my doe-eyed Sarah listening to friends, holding their secrets, soothing their pain, embracing their joys, all to her delight.

Her friends love her. And why not?

She has blossomed in all the ways I feared she might not. Maybe because I was the worried mother. Maybe because I projected my own awkwardness at that age onto her. My twenty-one-year-old Sarah has gone from being the girl last to sing at the Christmas party to the college girl center stage.

I tilt my head to one side.

I catch my breath with fascination and, ultimately, pride at how she is maneuvering.

This young woman is my kinda gal.

Funny, quick, gets the joke, makes the joke.

And she's a great confidante. Sarah is the one I go to when I need to talk to someone. She's very practical and does not suffer fools. It's only recently that I've shown her my ledge I sometimes stand on and let her help me off. And that's been a beautiful shift, one I was afraid to approach. I always felt I walked so closely to the lip of *my* mother's ledge that I knew way more than I could handle about her dark side. I never wanted my kids to know I even had one.

Last year, Sarah held my hand during a period of deep sadness I found myself wading through. She was my witness. She stood tall for me, and I let her.

She's brave. So very brave, for someone who was once so very timid.

My sweet, cautious Sarah.

The one Kurt, my third husband, and I had to pick up from sleepaway camp when she was nine, after just one night, because it was just too weird and scary for her to be with strangers.

The one who had a phase of eating only five different foods *for a long time*: butter noodles, grapes, cheesy toast, crackers with cream cheese (we called them "suns and moons"), and occasionally something green.

My Sarah, who could sleep only with lights on and would wake us up on a regular basis, convinced there was something or someone out her window. Kurt and I had to calm her and let her burrow into our big bed.

My Sarah, who just four years ago could not make up her mind about what color sheets to buy for her dorm, is now onstage, making choices, standing by them. I look around at the seats that are filling up in the school's theater—everyone there to see her show, to see her shine. That quiet, knowing way of hers, guiding her steps, lighting her path. How she has inside her the right thing to say, chooses just the right subtle approach, picks the right song to sing, the coolest arrangement to create.

She just knows.

I sit in the audience, her mother, witnessing who she is now, and in her present, I can see her bright future.

The Boy

Dear Jackson,

It is so hard to write about you.

At nineteen, you are kind of indescribable.

Mercurial, seeking, raging, gyrating side to side, you are hard to pin down.

And because I want you in my book of stories, I must try to find a way in.

I search for words.

My heart swells at your image.

And fills up all the space where words usually live.

The feelings are difficult to name.

I'm not sure they have a name.

Sometimes so big, words just don't get it.

You, even more than the other two, have hit a spot in me I never knew was there.

Raising a boy.

Being your mom.

Has opened me up to another side of things.

I am confused and refreshed by knowing you.

It's not just having a "boy."

It is you.

The kind of boy and man you are.

Love, Mom

✺ My Day with Jackson ✺

We decided to leave the house early, at 10:00 in the morning. At 10:20, he was still upstairs in his room, so I texted him.

"Feeling better? Ready to go?"

"Give me 20," he responded.

My son goes to the University of Southern California. USC. A hard school to get into. He got in on his audition and an SAT score that just eked over the required line and was just enough to make up for his very average GPA.

He is very talented.

It opens doors.

Having come up the same way, I don't worry about him the way other mothers might. I trust in his talent. Worry less about the specifics.

But I am his mom. And there are always specifics that need attending.

We were supposed to spend the day together. Jackson and

me. Him, home from school with another cold. The one that never really goes away and probably never will until he moves out of that petri dish of a college dorm he now happily calls home.

He'd been home from college the past three days with a throat infection and a fever. I took full advantage of having his ear. Reminded him—subtly, of course; trying not to be a nag—to get done some of the minutiae my sometimes distracted, often procrastinating son likes to skip over. Things that nineteen just can't seem to get to.

"Jackson," I said. "These are a few simple, though granted, tedious things you have to get together."

"Yeah, I know, Mom, I'm just so fucking busy."

"Since July?" I responded. "It's November! That's how long your license has been lost. And you need to put new tags on your car, too." My exasperated, serious tone almost made me laugh at how grown up I sounded.

"I know, I know, you're right . . ."

And to really make my point, I told him that he couldn't drive his car until he got himself to the DMV, and while he was at it, to pick up some much-needed new supplies—pants, socks, underwear, and a costume for his theater class—vitamins included, so maybe he could finally knock out this cold once and for all.

"Oh, and, *pleeeze*, let me help you register for that *one* general education class you need, just in case you ever decide finishing college might be a good idea.

"My day is wide open tomorrow," I added. "Let me take you around to get this all done."

He agreed, and as long as he was feeling better in the morning, we had a list to be crossed off.

It was a win-win.

Jackson gets his responsible mother to help him through those things that were always hard for him.

I get the sweetness of being near my son. That maternal charge, knowing I'm still needed.

As I was waiting for him to get ready, I decided to pick up my guitar in the kitchen and review the new song I'd been writing. I like to play in the kitchen. The acoustics are best in there.

Jackson blustered in. "Just a minute, Mom," he said. He's six foot three, and he kind of barrels around. "Let me make a quick sandwich, and we'll go."

"Okay, can I play you something?" I asked.

"Sure," he said, sitting down across from me at the kitchen island.

Jackson and I have music in common.

Of course, his musicianship has far surpassed mine at this point. He is an actual guitar player, whereas I'm infantile in my ability. But I've been playing the basics for many years as a way to write and sing. And he respects and encourages me.

As I do him.

His enthusiasm and his ability inspire me to want to play music. His joy when he listens to or plays music is infectious. It reminds me of that part of myself and makes me want to pick up my guitar, or play the piano, or write a song. And then share it with him.

He's a much better songwriter than me—my daughter Sarah is too. Jackson understands songs inherently and has a natural sense of their structure. He's just so talented. We often ask each other's advice on songs in progress, and share with and include each other.

For several years, I'd done gigs with the Forest Rangers, a band put together around the music we used on *Sons of Anarchy* by our music supervisor, Bob Thiele, Jr. We included songs used in the show's soundtrack, reinvented and sung by various artists. Audra Mae singing "Forever Young," Frankie Perez singing the *Sons* theme song, me singing Dusty Springfield's "Son of a Preacher Man," just to name a few. We played big venues, and whenever I could, I brought up Jackson to play in the band or to sing a few tunes with me. There's one song in particular we love to sing together: Steve Earle's "Come Home to Me." In 2014 my son got up and played it with me at the Stagecoach country music festival, an annual three-day event held at the Polo Empire Club in Indio, California, just outside of Palm Springs. Playing music with him onstage, it's almost indescribable. Definitely amazing.

I'm in another new band now because of him.

I'd taken a break from music after the end of *Sons*.

"Mom, you have to have a band," he said to me. "You have to be playing. Just go put a band together. You're happier like that."

And I did. I took his advice. I called up Bob, who's written for and played with Mavis Staples and Bonnie Raitt and produced two of my three solo records, and told him, "Let's start a band. Not a Katey Sagal band. A *band*." I didn't want my name on the project. I just wanted to be in the band.

We put together The Reluctant Apostles. A group of seasoned old friends, we'd all played together over the years. Bassist Davey Faragher, who's played with Cracker, Elvis Costello, and Sheryl Crow; keyboardist John Philip Shenale, who's played with Tori Amos and Jane's Addiction; drummer Michael Urbano, who's played with Cracker and John Hiatt; guitarist Billy Harvey, most recently having played with Patti Griffin; Bob; and me. And it's the most fun musical experience I've had since I made my first records in my twenties.

All because Jackson planted the seed.

So this is a familiar relationship for us, me asking him what he thinks of my new tune.

"I like parts of it," he said thoughtfully. "I think the melody could be a bit more interesting. It's kinda boring."

"Oh, okay, like what?"

Across from each other at the kitchen island, he grabbed my vintage Gibson acoustic (which I love so much, and which he's always trying to get his hands on) and played what I've been writing so much better than I did. Brought it to life. There I was, mesmerized by his ease with the instrument, reminding me why I love the sound of this guitar, taking me back to my most familiar, safe place.

Playing music.

He helped me to expand the melody over chords I couldn't play. When he played them, I just naturally sang more interesting notes, and, as we always do, we fell into a groove. We harmonize easily—share the gift, like I shared the gift with my mom all those many years ago when she taught me to play her old Martin guitar from Burl Ives. My fondest memories of my mom and me are now some of the sweetest moments I share with this son of mine. Which makes them all the sweeter.

We played and ate for a while and then headed out on our day of errands. Sitting mostly in silence, which is how we like it, because it's so easy for us to just be together.

I love all three of my kids uniquely, each one.

My firstborn, Sarah, holds that honored position, and she's exceptional. Individual. My number one child. She's the one who showed me the ropes and opened my heart so deep and wide.

My third child is also a girl: sweet, complex Esmé. Holds the sometimes most-favored but oftentimes most-neglected baby spot, and she will forever be my last child, my baby girl. Her special place.

And then there is my son.

That cliché about mothers and sons is without a doubt the real deal with us. We have a very special bond, me and this kid.

I have two girls and one boy.

We call him "the boy."

And this boy of mine, Jackson, like most of the men I have fallen in love with in my life, has me wrapped. Only the mother of a son might know what I mean.

I once read an anonymous quote: "There has never been, nor will there ever be, anything quite so special as the love between a mother and a son."

Yep, that about sums it up.

Of the three, I'd have to say he is my "old soul" child. (Esmé appears to be clairvoyant, but I'm not sure that constitutes an old soul.) Like I was at his age, he is wise beyond his years, empathetic to a fault, has very few filters, and wears his heart on his sleeve.

He is very special. I knew it the minute I laid eyes on him.

Wise, and calm, and tortured by all that was, even as a child, he knew more than I saw, all that I saw, even before I did.

He came second.

And right away, I could feel a soulful depth and stillness about his energy. (Of course, he's a musician.) Might be because, with the second, I was more relaxed during the time we shared space, but for whatever reason, he came in Zen-like. This child latched onto my breast, like he knew where he was going, and he would languish there for hours, soaking me in with his big, brown eyes, and looking at me confused when he'd drank me dry, and it was time to let go. (At nineteen, he still loves the comforts of home, and I imagine he may always be my one that never quite leaves.)

Jackson was intuitive and empathetic, even as a small child. As a four-year-old, he could sense if things were awry and slip into your lap, nestle into your neck, and let you know he could feel your pain and that you were loved. Sensitive to subtle shifts of mood, sometimes causing him pain and discomfort, he is able to read the room, fortunately or unfortunately—however you choose to look at it.

Just like his mom.

He'd rather pound his drums, play his guitar or his piano, space out in front of the TV, practicing or writing, not talking.

I so get him.

Sometimes we go to the movies in the middle of the day, sit in the theater together, eating popcorn, not talking.

He's never much liked school, even though, if he ever gave a shit about it, he'd ace it. It's never been about brainpower. He's just a guy who is naturally good at a few specific things and has always known where his heart is and which direction this life is taking him. He prefers to stick to those passions of his heart.

The lesson that Kurt and I most try to pass on to him (more like shove down his throat) is that there is merit in doing those things you don't want to do. Taking action and working the muscle required to finish an unmotivating task is a skill that serves us almost more than the accomplishment itself. It's the magic tool.

Our son is learning in his own time. I feel his attention and genuine appreciation for my ear and words of motherly advice. But only when asked.

What I've learned with Jackson, like I've learned with most men, is to not give advice until I'm asked. Or at least I know to ask him first, before just shoving the maternal advice his way.

Would you like to hear my opinion?

Would you like some advice?

Sometimes he says no.

But more times than not, when I approach it that way, he wants to hear it.

He loves his mom.

I don't bug him. If he needs something, he'll ask.

He's reminded me how to keep it simple. Stick to the topic rather than dart around.

Conversation with Jackson is efficient. He fills me in, gives me a "What do you think?"

I tell him.

Jackson doesn't push back. My daughters, as many women do, push back. Weigh all sides, indulge in the pros and cons. It's more about process than outcome.

I do it too. Not so much about the solution as being heard and reasoning things out.

Jackson likes to get to the answer.

Being the mother of a boy has taught me more about men than any of those years hanging with the guys or any of my three marriages.

Jackson came downstairs one morning, the summer before college. It had been a big decision for him to go to USC and not to just play music. Maybe go to Nashville. Stay with his band. He looked slumpy. Tired. Maybe sad.

"Are you second-guessing your decision to go to USC?" I asked.

"No," he sighed. "I know it's the right thing to do. I'm really kind of upset about my band. It's busting up."

"That must be hard, honey." I was surprised. "You guys have been so tight."

This was the first I'd heard that the band he'd spent the last two years forming, investing in, and recording and performing with was in a state of confusion. He'd felt so close to them, as you

do in your first band. Put all his eggs in that basket. And really loved making music with them.

I needed to listen.

When it fell apart, Jackson didn't really understand why. He was heartbroken. He'd given all of the power to these other people, felt that he was musically lost without them, didn't understand how good he was on his own. It was a big confidence lesson for him.

But, for a while, until he got the lesson, it was a touchy situation.

I wanted to give him tons of advice. I tried. But it was like an open sore. The more I pressed, the more it hurt him.

Finally, I got that I couldn't just tell him how great he was. He had to find his way to this knowledge on his own. And from there, I got the big one. It's kind of like the overall rule with children: you just have to slow down because they need the time to learn their lessons at their own pace. It's hard because it's all stuff that you know already.

But they have to get it for themselves.

It took him awhile to get it. During that time, my son felt intermittently lost and struggled to find his voice. So he was very, very quiet. Which was hard for me. But I kept still, heeding my own advice that too much chatter would clutter his healing.

Now what I observe in his behavior comes only with time.

He is able to hold hurt and happiness in the same moment, in the same heart, stand in the face of it. Running into painful memories and being able to keep them right sized. He learned the lesson of fortitude and, at twenty, is inching his way toward self-reliance.

And all of this has started to form a deeper artistic self.

A voice that he's finally starting to hear again.

That intuitive voice that he was born with, that he's now remembering, as we do on the other side of adolescence.

I'm proud of him, my boy.

Esmé, the Teacher

Esmé is my amazing third child.

Esmé was born via surrogate—not so unusual these days, but ten years ago, when we began the process, that definitely wasn't the case.

The fact that Kurt and I wanted to pursue having a child together was also different, at least for us. It wasn't something we had intended when we got married on October 2, 2004.

I was already a full family when we got together. Sarah was six and a half, and Jackson was five. Kurt is six years younger than me, and at the time, he was childless and okay with that. He thought he'd never have children. It was not something he'd had a strong desire for or had envisioned for himself.

But I felt Kurt's heart grow bigger from stepparenting Sarah and Jackson. We took the kids to a ranch up in Santa Barbara. No phones. No TV. We shared a big room with the two of us and the two of them. We played board games and went horseback riding. I believe, without the distraction of technology, allowing himself to be one with the silence of his heart, Kurt experienced an internal shift. I could feel it.

Like he says now, the process of joining our family opened his eyes to the idea of us having a child together. And for me, that was kind of a no-brainer, knowing how having my children made me love in a way I never thought possible—and wanting him to know that too. How, why, would I deny that to this man I loved so deeply?

About five years into my relationship with Kurt, we both had the thought that a child together would make sense, would complete our unit, would be an adventure we would like to take. We circled the conversation with questions of "Is it even possible?"

We decided to find out.

As we do most things, we put it in motion and told ourselves, "If it's meant to be, it will."

I could no longer carry a child, given previous complications. And Kurt couldn't remember having ever knocked up anyone. So our first step was to explore adoption. We met with an adoption attorney. I made these big books about our family that we were going to send to birth mothers.

Here's the frustrating thing about private adoption. You can't ask the birth mothers any questions. "Do you drink? Are you taking vitamins? Are you on drugs?" But they can ask *you* questions. They have to pick you. Kurt and I are not very good at subtlety or silence. Nobody was choosing us.

At a certain point, I said let's go down the adoption road *and* the surrogacy road, and see what happens first. He agreed. (Privately, I think he had an urge to pass on his genetics.)

We explored surrogacy and found it to be a much easier, less stressful approach. There were a few hurdles that needed jumping, but we persevered.

Esmé's inception was rocky.

Lots of science.

In the process of creating embryos, we were able to manifest only two. One and a half, really, as only one embryo appeared strong enough to survive. Usually during the process of in vitro fertilization, you hope for at least a half dozen viable embryos to implant, with the hope that at least one will survive. With Esmé, we had a "one-shot" chance. Very low odds for survival.

We said to ourselves, "We will not go through all of this again."

If this was meant to be, it would happen.

If not, we were prepared to let go.

We would read it as a sign that we had enough family, and we would be satisfied. Our one and a half viable embryos were implanted in our surrogate, and our viable option clung on. Through a series of unusual and seemingly miraculous outcomes, our youngest miracle, Esmé, came to be and made her way to us.

I'd had a little bit of apprehension from the conception. It was so different from having a baby grow inside my own body. When I'd been pregnant, I'd known what vitamins I was taking, and I'd known what the doctor said at my appointments. Without having that control over the process, we felt a need to make sure the mom was healthy, and to hear what the doctors had to say. We were fortunate to have our surrogate close by, and Kurt and I went to every doctor's appointment with her. And we were in the hospital room when Esmé was born, on January 10, 2007. It may have been the quickest delivery ever. Our surrogate dilated and gave birth in twenty minutes. We had special music picked out for the occasion, but then we couldn't get the iPod to play! And the music that was on instead was Cypress Hill Gang's "(Rap) Superstar," which wasn't meant to be playing. All of a sudden, before we could change the music, out came Esmé.

The nurse immediately put Esmé on me. I wasn't sure what to expect because I'd only had children that came out of me. But I put her on my breast, and she latched on, and it was amazing. And then Kurt took her and cleaned her up. We stayed with her in the hospital for two days, because she was a little bit jaundiced, and then we brought her home. I was nervous about what it would be like. It wasn't that I ever doubted that she was my daughter. But the bonding process was a bit different from if I'd carried her inside of my body for nine months, with our hearts beating together. Rather than the continuation of that connection, it was a growing love, but it was strong from the beginning. I've always thought it probably felt more like being the dad, getting to know the baby after her birth. Love at first sight, instead of love at first heartbeat.

And so, at fifty-two, I became a mom again. (That experience alone, I could probably write a whole book on.)

Esmé arrived with a heart so big it can break at the slightest shift in the tone or facial expressions of those around her and a busy, anxious brain. Extremely sensitive, she came into this life with few filters. She explodes at the slightest adjustment but wraps you in hugs when no one else could even see you needed one.

Since she was four, we've been asked the question "What's up with Esmé?"

"What is up with Esmé is that she is different," was my response at the time, and it remains my response now. "What's wrong with that?"

It's okay to be different.

Different has always worked for me.

She, of all three of my kids, is the strongest example of all the differences that both Kurt and I exhibited as kids, when such behavior was dealt with in the worst ways. We had big emotions. We were prone to high anxiety. Those "Shut it down, Sarah Bernhardt" comments from my father because I cried at the slightest provocation. Rather than being understood, our emotionality was a hindrance to be toned down, so we learned to suppress. With food. With, eventually, booze and work. But Kurt and I have done enough personal work that when we had Esmé, we realized right away that her different way of seeing the world was an opportunity and a blessing. We just had to find a key to her. She is like us in so many ways. Which makes the similarities hard to look at sometimes. But that's all about us, not her.

She has always awed us.

And frustrated us.

From her beginnings, to her current regimen, it's all been "different."

Esmé is amazing, challenging, exhausting, enlightening, and forces me to live in the present even more intensely than I did before, which I like.

And now, at this stage in my life, she is my constant spiritual teacher.

Children are the teachers that parents can never find—until they have children.

The lessons they bring are the eye-opening, revelatory kind that happen only through that familial bond. You learn different things from each one. About yourself, about your parental relationships, about your reactions and responses to the world.

Esmé came with a boatload for both of us.

Our little hurricane.

The most demonstrative of all my children, at a very young age she showed concern and compassion for anything breathing. Human or animal. Extremely tactile, she'd physically glue herself to anyone or anything she loved. And she loves a lot. She likes to be squeezed and cuddled tightly so she can really feel it.

The chaotic motion of her brain means she can erupt with frustration and doesn't always play well with others her own age. Things have to be a certain way for her to remain calm. It took us the first five years of her life to figure out these things. With the help of school shadows and behaviorists, we started to unlock what makes Esmé tick.

Her emotional life mimicked both Kurt's and mine: a huge heart and an extra helping of anxiety. She had unbearable tantrums, mood swings, and meltdowns that left us bewildered and frightened.

"What the fuck *is* up with Esmé?" people asked.

Now we also wondered.

"Nothing," we kept hoping.

"She'll grow out of it," we said.

Just a willful child.

"It's good to have a girl with spunk," people commented.

Yeah, my ass.

Her "spunk" was blowing shit up and was in danger of taking up all the space in the house.

The diagnosis of kids is a slippery slope.

What is brain chemistry? What is a defiant brat?

If I'd ever acted out the way our youngest was, I'd have been properly spanked, not allowed to ride my bike for a week, lost my TV privileges, and that would have been it. I'd have thought twice before throwing my cereal on the floor again.

Not so with Esmé.

Punishment for bad behavior has never prevented the exact same fucking behavior from reoccurring.

Over and over.

It was like Groundhog Day—day after day.

The hard part was watching her try to manage the constant chatter in her head so that she could find a quieter place. We came to observe that her obsessions for certain activities simplified her complications. Repetitive activities that focused her attention. Watching her iPad worked (we now call it "screen time," and it's monitored), snail hunting worked for a while (now it's lizards). And she's really good at it and can do it for hours.

At six the diagnosis process began. Her first psych evaluation and a result:

ADHD, a bit of dyslexia, a possible mood disorder.

"Oh shit. She's not just misbehaving. She's doing the best she can to deal with what she's been given," we said. "Okay, so maybe there *is* something up with Esmé."

Something that might require medication, so she can stop spinning, flailing, forever trying to jump out of her own skin. Medication, we struggled with but ultimately gave in to. And stand by. I could go into lengthy descriptions of medicines and outcomes, but I won't. Medical interventions, as well as behavioral modifications, have been working for our little hurricane. By no means a straight line, adjustments and consistent monitoring are the norm for us, and her, but the improvements have been undeniable.

She has Mom's and Dad's artistic temperaments. At the end of third grade, her school sent home her artwork, and it's fantastic. We framed them all. She's very much her own person with her own interests. We watch the occasional *SpongeBob SquarePants*, but mostly she wants to watch the National Geographic Channel and animal documentaries. She loves all the gory details there are to know about animals and insects. She's fascinating, and she has a great vocabulary, even though she sometimes mixes up her words. But we always know what she means.

Esmé is super-intuitive smart. I think it's because people with anxious brains tend to be extra observant, and she definitely is. I wouldn't go so far as to use the "pseudo-scientific new age concept indigo child," but sometimes I think she's supernatural.

The last time we went to our house in Idaho, she planted a fairy garden because she believes in fairies. Kurt tells her all the time that Santa Claus, the Easter Bunny, and fairies are all real, as long as you believe in them, and so far, she still does. With so much conviction, she might be right.

Lying on Mom and Dad's bed one night, turning off our usual bedtime documentary, she gives me a deep look.

"Let's talk. You know, Mommy, ghosts and aliens are real. And if you're not afraid of them they won't get mad and hurt you. And, also, the soul never dies."

"I believe that about the soul," I say.

"No, it's true."

How does she know that? I wonder.

"How do you know that? *I* know that, but how do you know that? Did somebody tell you that?"

"No, Mom, it's just true."

Like I've learned with all my kids, I believe and agree, shut up and listen, and hope they'll talk some more.

The wisdom of "the soul never dies" out of my nine-year-old blue-eyed beauty is something we've become accustomed to. She's in touch with things.

She's now learning to shift gears smoothly. She likes advance warning, likes to know what happens next, is more comfortable having her life organized. Esmé remains calm when she knows the plan. She'll ask me in advance what's going to happen.

"Okay, Mom, tell me the plan again," she'll ask for the fifth time. (I've lovingly started calling her "Dory.")

"Okay, the plan is you wake up, teach imaginary school in your room for fifteen minutes, get dressed, brush your teeth, eat breakfast, snuggle with Mom and Dad, head out the door for school," I say every day.

"Okay," she says, finding comfort.

We use timers in our house. For example, before dinner, she'll have an hour of reading and an hour of screen time. We set the timer, so she'll know how much time before the end of each activity, and then dinner.

Those timers are good for all of our arty, easily distracted brains.

It turns out we all like to know the plan.

After dinner, we do a thing we call "good vibes," where Esmé plays a song or two on the piano, to say good night to the house. Lately it's been songs that she writes, which, of course, thrills us to no end.

Then it's bath time, usually with Mom. We give each other a salt scrub and a good sponging. She calls it giving a beauty treatment. She'd rather scrub than be scrubbed.

If we have extra time, we play a game of UNO. Read three books with Mom and Dad, with Esmé holding on to her purple bunny and "Fiddle Pup."

And then, our favorite time of day: Mom, Dad, and Esmé say their prayers. I never said prayers as a kid. Kurt did because he was Catholic and had to. Spirituality was something that we both came to later in life, and separate from our families, but it has become very important to us. We'd like to be able to say that we were Esmé's example of living a spiritual life, and we brought spirituality to her, but the truth is, she's the source. Neither Kurt nor I can quite remember when or how it began, but we both know for sure that it was her idea to start saying prayers. It was explained to us early on that kids with "stuff" need a strong spiritual life. They need that trust in a power greater than themselves. And Esmé has that in spades.

We each take turns. Esmé starts.

"Dear God, thank you for the day I had," she says. "Thank you for all the fun in my life."

And then, a minimum of three nights out of the week, she'll say something wizard-like, as with her musings on the soul, which gets Kurt and me bawling immediately.

"Tears of joy," her daddy tells her when she sees him crying.

Then Daddy says his prayers. Every night he thanks Esmé for the lessons he's learning from her.

And then I say mine. We all start, "Thank you for the day I had."

Then it's calm-down time, and we have a quick meditation.

What heals her so much is all the love she feels from her parents. It helps her to stay connected, and, really, it helps all of us to stay connected to one another and our higher selves. What started out for our family as a mystery because there was such a different way of seeing the world through Esmé's eyes has now become a blessing.

Esmé is our teacher.

clinic, Rasma as my support, probably after school. (I don't really remember.) The doctor sucked out my baby. I was young and didn't feel any consequence.

Rasma took me to a friend's house, so I could recoup from my evacuation away from my parents' eyes. She lay next to me in a twin bed in the back room. We drank Southern Comfort and giggled, relieved that my parents were none the wiser.

There was another one aborted maybe a year after the first one. I can say that, at the time, it was, to me, my only option. I treated the procedures as casually as I had treated my body, which is what had gotten me there in the first place.

I was sleepwalking.

It was only after the successful arrival of my oldest child that I gave those first two a thought—and a good cry. I am pro-choice, yet my behavior at sixteen and then again at seventeen had nothing to do with making a choice. There was no choice about it. Just an instinctual urge to make the potential source of inconvenience and trouble go away.

Looking back, I reflect on who I was at that time. I had already taken flight from day-to-day goings-on into a haze of diet pills and red wine. I was shy, overweight, manly (Daddy's word, not mine!), and once I was fueled up with a bit of speed and wine from a jug, I could turn on the girly flirty bit and take whatever was offered up.

I gave my body recklessly.

So did my friends. We were all about it.

As for women's movement chatter, we misinterpreted what it meant to be living liberal.

On Mothering

I am the mother of three children.

Three living children.

I've carried more . . .

In my teens, there were "accidents." Lazy, selfish accidents. And terminations without question or remorse.

I was sixteen years old. My weight was an issue, and I was giving away my body as a way to cover that up. (I was that fat girl who, if you looked at me twice, I'd do it with you.) Runnin' with Rasma, my absolutely beautiful best friend: tall, chestnut hair, green eyes. I think even *I* had a crush on her, as did every guy that I ended up fucking.

Just like that, I was late. My unexpected surprise was from someone I thought was my boyfriend, but that would have been news to him.

Anyway, somehow I was pregnant. I ended up in a free

We lived stupid.

STDs, free clinic visits for antibiotics, Kwell lotion. Sometimes weekly visits, always on a regular basis . . .

In my twenties, I got married. Freddie Beckmeier and I never got pregnant.

In my thirties, I got married again, to Jack White. Before we got married, we couldn't *stop* getting pregnant. After just three short months, I was knocked up. We miscarried. Within the next three months, knocked up again.

Ruby.

A baby girl. Stillborn.

Now I am one mother.

With three children.

I am a very different mother to each one of them. Not in all ways, but my mothering is not a one-size-fits-all type of mothering. And they are not one-size-fits-all kids. Sarah likes to talk a lot, mull things over, voice her opinions. She likes to have discussion. She's opinionated, and she needs an ear. It's not difficult because she's so interesting. She likes to be with people more than alone. She's not as solitary as her younger brother, Jackson. He also likes to have his mother's ear, but he's much more to the point. He wants feedback, but only when he asks. Esmé, the youngest, requires more hugs than the other two (but she also gives more) and a lot more physical attention.

We have our share of "Our family never does that."

And "That's just so us."

We all tend to share a wry sense of humor. And together we can all share a good joke. But, for example, Sarah finds it easy to laugh at herself, whereas Jackson tends to take it all to heart. He can dish it out, but he can't always take it. Esmé, being surrounded by older siblings and a household filled with doting adults, has that "Look at me!" baby thing and always wants to show she can get the joke.

What has worked for one has never worked for all, aside from the basics: manners, kindness, giving back.

They have all had different requirements, but there were also ways in which I have parented them similarly.

I've made every mistake a parent could possibly make. That's how I've learned, through trial and error, oftentimes by doing the wrong thing first. None of them came with a how-to parenting book, as no kid does.

I've shoved my opinions down their throats. I've kept them very close. I've coddled them and done more for them, maybe, than I should have. I've practically taken their baby steps for them. I'm still trying to undo that.

I've been distracted by work, especially when I was a single mom trying to keep all the balls in the air.

My children, finally, taught me to listen. The lessons I'm learning now, as the parent of a twenty-two-year-old and a twenty-year-old, are about just being there for them.

They are all affected by my disappointment in their occasional poor choices. But it doesn't stop them from sharing them with me. They know I'll be reasonable—or at least strive for that.

I give them my attention.

They tell me how they feel. Not always the circumstances of their lives, I'm sure, but how they feel.

When they are lost.

When they are overwhelmed.

When they are triumphant and proud.

I stop for them.

I sit on my hands.

I hold my tongue.

I stifle my opinions, so they'll keep coming back, keep talking.

To an open heart.

I've always told them to ask for what they want in life. You may not get it, but you should always ask.

When I became a parent, I vowed not to be like my parents. For my parents, having kids was different than having kids was for me. I was born on the tail end of "Children should be seen and not heard." So I can't wholeheartedly throw blame on my folks for not listening very well. I wasn't supposed to have a voice. So what did they know?

They half-assed heard me. It was selective. Through their own shit opinions about themselves. I learned how to talk really fast, get to the fucking point, before a door slammed, before their eyes rolled, or mine started welling up.

I'd exaggerate.

I'd dramatize.

I learned to be a really good liar. About things I shouldn't have had to lie about.

Who my friends were, or where I was going, or where I'd been the night before. But just in case what *I* thought was normal wasn't. And, never quite sure if the truth would set a fire, I'd lie. Just in case.

In my years of recovery, I've heard a lot about always having a plan B. Didn't have to tell me that. Maybe I didn't have a plan B in my career. But I grew up always having a plan B: an escape hatch, a lie to keep me safe.

As the oldest of five kids, my position would diminish with each new arrival. It's tough to share the top spot, especially when there wasn't a large reservoir to begin with. I always felt the squeeze and the burden we put on my mom. I'd watch her shrink, just a little bit, under the weight of one more mouth to feed, one more dream to scratch off her list as time ran thin, with all those diapers and bottles and dreams that drowned out her own.

So I give what I had hoped to receive.

I didn't know what it meant to really commit until I had my children. Marriage always had its exits, particularly in the generation in which I grew up, where everyone seemed to get divorced. With children, it's forever. You work it out. That's what it means to love.

It always fills me up, gives me more: energy, life, a reason to stand tall, not shrink or deplete.

I always say my kids saved my life. Really what I mean is: they gave me life.

Being their mom has helped me to know what my parents must have felt for me. It makes me certain that at one time, it was love like that. Even if my parents couldn't always show it.

I couldn't wait to have my kids (when it was time to have them).

No amount of career success has impressed me the way I was impressed by giving birth. That was miraculous. That was an achievement I could clock and be proud of.

My mother always had to have help. She was in bed a lot. I also have always had help. Because I was working, I had to find a way to do both things. That was the difference between my mother and me. I was going to find a way to have a job, a good marriage, and a family. That's why it took so long to let go of my marriage to the father of my first two kids, because my conviction was to have a solid marriage and family life. So I was going to make it one. Only in hindsight can I see that I had to let go of that family ideal to get to where I am now.

The other thing I've done differently from my parents is this: I've slowly revealed to them myself and the realities of my life, as they were the appropriate age. When you raise children, you spend so much of your time protecting them from any and all evil forces in the world. I remember the day when, in response to "That's not fair," I started to tell them, "You know what? The world's not fair. You're right. And you've got to deal with it."

There also comes a time when I let them know I've had a rough go of it too. I got sober before I had my kids. They'd always known I didn't drink because I was allergic to alcohol. They didn't know the gory details. Now the older two do. I revealed it slowly.

The best we can do is to be the example. Live our lives well and if it's supposed to rub off, it will.

When I first became a mom, I unfairly expected myself to be all things to all of my kids. What I've learned is that you find

your strong suit and don't expect yourself to have all bases covered. I was never a good playdate or silly-games-playing mom.
I liked Legos and coloring, board games, and puzzles. But I was
not great at make-believe and tea parties, dolls and playing house.
I'm the one you come to for advice. I'm kind and nurturing, and
good with life lessons and compassion regarding affairs of the
heart, and so on. As with most things in life, I've learned this
about myself in hindsight.

The benefits are profoundly revealed in the more relaxed
way I parent my third child, Esmé. I've let go of my opinions on
what I should be doing that I'm not.

I play to my strengths and parcel out whatever else she needs
to others who do it better: a kind babysitter, a doting aunt, the
housekeeper, the nanny, the neighbor.

So dare to lower your expectations on the parenting front.

Stop being so anal about doing shit perfectly.

And get happier kids, because you're not such a neurotic
mess.

You'll actually be present, and your kids will be too!

Beautiful Man

Kurt and I met in the spring of 2001. I was a year into my separation from my second husband, Jack. I'd just filed for divorce and was spending all my free time either with my kids or in a twelve-step room.

That's where he was.

In a room.

The first time I noticed him was . . . simply the first time I noticed him, although he'd apparently been going to this particular meeting for a while. I'd never seen him there before. Or in any of the rooms I frequented.

Until the day I did.

Maybe he'd been hiding in the back. Or maybe the fog that had covered my life throughout the traumatic last two years of my previous marriage was finally lifting. Maybe I could just see again.

And I liked what I saw.

Kurt was the speaker at the meeting that day. He was very handsome. And I was struck by how genuine he was in his recovery share. He felt grounded, warm, smart, and spiritual. Funny with edge. I remember thinking, *Who is that?*

He was wearing workout clothes and was in great shape, so my first assumption was that he must be a trainer. Handsome, buff dudes in Hollywood, wearing sweat suits, tend to be that. And just as quickly, there went my skeptical mind: *Even though he's hot, I'm not really interested in the athletic type.*

I didn't think much more about it.

But he spoke to me that day while getting cups of coffee in the back of the room.

"I liked your share," I said.

We stumbled about with the milk and sweeteners, stirring our coffees, making nothing talk. But he was looking at me with interest. I was so preoccupied by my personal life at the time, I couldn't really see men as men, or as in maybe-interested-in-me kind of men.

But he was.

I think.

"Could we go get coffee sometime after the meeting?" he asked.

A vague request. But the meeting was weekly, so I knew I'd see him again.

"Yes," I said.

I left the room that afternoon and didn't go back to that meeting for another four months. (It was a Saturday group, and the kids had soccer practice on Saturdays; I just couldn't get there.) I'd been flattened by my past romantic life and my separation. The tragedy of breaking up a family was the biggest hurdle for me. Coming from my own noncohesive tribe, I had fortified myself with the notion that once I had my own kids—a safe harbor, for them and for me—all would be right with the world. The illusion of my "happy home" was the most difficult of my denials to overcome. But my denial about the problems in my marriage had finally lifted.

I'd started going to Al-Anon, a twelve-step program for the families and friends of those affected by the disease of alcoholism, whether the person is actively drinking or not. I'd had numerous relationships with alcoholics, including my marriage to Jack, who legitimately tried to stay sober throughout our marriage. Me being the common denominator in all those relationships, I finally realized I could work only on myself, I qualified to be in Al-Anon and related to what I heard in its rooms.

There is a piece of me that "needs to be needed." Picking up the broken parts pulls me in and ensures I'll stay. That part of me is so imbedded in my DNA, I sleepwalk into the caretaker spot, even while fully intending *not to do that*. Putting myself back into the frustratingly simplistic position of trying to save my dying mother, or please my unpleasable father, through my current adult relationships and interactions. I was repeating my patterns once again in my marriage.

My history would make me lock in on relationships where I felt needed.

I'm not a quitter.

I'll never let you go until you fucking get better!

That piece seems empathetic but is actually kind of pathetic. Because I wasn't letting the other person have the dignity of his or her own experience. Plus, I'd get suffocated in the process, as is inevitable when playing that role.

Other than the lessons of my own recovery journey from drugs and alcohol, unraveling this piece of my puzzling psyche has been the most informative and insidious one to stumble through.

It's hard to recognize.

You don't just "never do it again."

There are no hard and fast rules, like "Just say no."

Nothing like that.

I grew up feeling indispensable in regards to my parents' happiness. The message was passed down that I could save my mother's life, smooth out the edges of my father's volatile moods, make it a good day or a bad day.

That I was powerful.

And responsible.

And worthless—if I failed at saving your ass or saving your face, never getting it quite right, letting you down, or never reaching high enough to keep anyone satisfied.

And yet I was always indispensable because "Your love for me keeps me going."

I gave you a reason to live. Which gave *me* a reason to live.

It is an in-process, complicated frame of mind—a way of being that requires daily weeding through. Because this piece of me is at my core. Always there. And it requires a constant maintenance of the tricky maneuvering between loving and smothering. Differentiating between what is mine and what is yours.

My then-ending marriage provided the bottom I needed.

I climbed slowly up out of the pit.

I had learned how to take better care of myself, instead of just my husband, and that's what I was doing.

That, and single parenting four- and six-year-old Jackson and Sarah.

In the four months that followed that afternoon, I thought about the handsome guy I'd met after his share. Told myself I should get to that Saturday meeting soon, so we could "go get coffee."

I wondered if he had a job. Because, I thought, if I were to have coffee with him, and if I were to find him interesting, I might get sucked into something lustful that might lead to something involved, and once again, I'd be shackled by my heart without having all the facts first.

Welcome to my brain! Always ten steps ahead of where I actually am. It's something I work on constantly: Being. Where. I. Am.

It's my struggle.

Anyway . . .

I've never been anything but happily self-supporting. And I had been the primary breadwinner in past relationships, and I was determined to not get into that position ever again. Even on a date. A job was required of anyone I might consider.

I thought if handsome Kurt might be asking me on a date, I would go, but only if he had a job. And not just a freelance kind of job. A real one. With a paycheck. Oh, and I was burnt on musicians, so that, too, would mean a no-go as far as I was concerned.

As Kurt has explained to me since, he never would have pursued even coffee with me unless he'd had a job. And not just any job: a job involving his heart's desire. He, too, had experienced not being true to himself and was on his own path of following his heart and knowing where he was. "A man's self-worth is reliant on and wrapped up in what he does," said wise Kurt once.

And that's not all about money.

Being true to oneself. Taking care of business. Being able to *take care of*.

And if a "he" doesn't feel right about "his place" (and I don't mean because of how many pennies are in his pocket), and you are in "your right place" (and making shitloads of dough—okay, it does have a bit to do with that. Truth!), he will soon hate himself. And guess what? He will tear you down and spit you out for making him feel so bad about himself, unconsciously of course. That has been my experience.

When I went back to the Saturday meeting, Kurt was there. He caught me by the coffeepot again.

"Where have you been?" he asked.

"Kids," I said.

His hands were shaking.

Too much coffee? Nervous to be talking to me? Not sure, but I noted it as he asked for my number.

Damn, he was handsome!

He called that week, and I'm pretty sure that I asked him, "So, what do you do? Are you a trainer?"

Kurt laughed. "No, I'm a writer," he said.

(Sigh of relief.)

"I usually work out after that meeting," he continued.

"What do you write?" I asked.

"Movies that haven't been made, but now I'm on staff for a television series called *The Shield*."

(Huge sigh of relief: the guy gets a paycheck. I can have coffee with him!)

We made a date for the next Saturday.

On the day, it was raining.

I was suddenly nervous about being alone with handsome Kurt, mostly because I didn't trust my man picker. He could have been one of those star-fucking dirtbags I'd so far managed to skirt. Or he could have been a "fixer-upper," and I might have fallen for him, once again mistaking red flags for minor baggage that I could "patch up," as had been my pattern in the past. Always a sucker for a good-looking man. Blinded, I should say.

My penchant for broken dudes, and the comforting familiarity of trying to fix them, had become glaringly clear through the inventory process in all my recovery rooms. I was determined to keep my eyes open. Not that anyone I might meet in a twelve-step room wouldn't come with shit, myself included. But it's the way you handle your stuff that makes all the difference.

I took a chaperone on my coffee date with Kurt: my sponsor, Marjorie. I loved her so dearly. She taught me by example how to see the glass as half full. Not in an airy-fairy, rose-colored-glasses kind of way. She could call bullshit when she saw it. But at the same time, she'd find the best in any given situation. She neither wallowed nor worried (after years of recovery). I was still just rebounding from years of wallow and worry, so she would be my eyes and ears on this first "hello" with Kurt. In case he was nuts, I'd have a way out with the claim "We have to be somewhere."

What struck me most was his warmth.

He told us about himself without us having to dig and honestly offered himself up.

A few gory details about his past and how he found himself in the rooms. This did not alarm me. It's how we do it with each other. It's alcoholicspeak. He'd had food addictions, alcohol and drug addictions, been married and divorced, was sober ten years. He had been an actor (*Yikes*, I thought, *not into that*) but was now a writer (*Thank God. Much better!*).

He asked about me, my kids, my path. And he really listened.

I felt paid attention to. It was nice.

At some point, Marjorie squeezed my knee under the table and grinned one of her wry grins, a confirmation and a nod that he was all right. And then, I don't remember her saying goodbye. She was just gone.

And it was just us.

In the coffee shop. And the rain. For the next three hours.

*   *   *

It all started with that meeting at a coffee shop on an ordinary Saturday in the rain. I was surprised how quickly I felt at home with him. Kindred, new, yet old. Like we'd met before, like I'd always known him, or he'd finally found me again. Exactly one month after our first coffee date, during which we kept postponing the inevitable, we were lying together, his body close to mine.

Don't move a muscle kept running through my brain, because I wasn't used to the intimacy of such stillness.

He didn't.

I didn't.

The closeness of that small action, so unlike what I'd known and where I'd been.

His strong arms relaxing around my waist, pulling me close.

His solid, warm breath on my neck, in and out, slow, consistent, without hesitation, not letting me go.

"I'm here," he whispered. "Be with me."

He held my hand.

It stayed firmly in mine, no question.

No clasping and unclasping.

It was like nothing I'd known before.

Reciprocated, intentional, we dove in.

I called him "the unbroken man."

At last.

"Beautiful man."

Kind, open, with integrity and sobriety.

We spoke the same speak.

At last.

Bumps did not deter us: children to meet, logistics to figure out, things to untangle. As we got more serious—and it clearly couldn't get more serious without involving my children—if there was any hesitation on his part, it was just to take a breath to make sure he could handle what would be required being with a woman with children.

Kurt took it on, and he has been fantastic with them.

There are tricky waters to navigate with the confusion of loyalties for little people. And he moved, as he does with most things, at a slow, methodical pace. This was his subtle way of figuring out if he could do it. Little by little, he was in. I watched Kurt fall in love with not only me but also the children he now calls his own. He wanted to give them the time to know him. Not forcing himself on them, allowing them room for the extra adult who would now love them too. Sarah and Jackson's dad continues to be a strong presence in their lives, and in ours. We are in balance.

Nothing could undo us.

No doubt, or fear, or circumstance could douse us.

We silenced everything.

Just kept moving forward.

You, Kurt, were what I thought love should be.

But you, my darling, with our lust as hot as our hearts, were what I had lost faith in ever finding. I thought it was only in the movies or for other people. Your reassuring gaze, your appreciation for having found me, falling for me.

You'd say, "I'm the lucky one."

That was fifteen years ago.

And I'm the lucky one, still.

Jane Fonda Famous

After a long process, I decided to wear the orange dress to the Golden Globe Awards in 2011. I had an orange one, a red one, and a black one to choose from. My stylist had brought me all of these different options, and we'd narrowed it down to three, and I'd gone to fittings for all of them. But then, none of us, meaning my team—my publicist, my manager, my stylist, or my hair and makeup people—could make a decision. Finally, it was five minutes until I had to walk out the door.

We chose the orange one.

I was so happy. It had been my first choice, and it was definitely the boldest. But there had been this chorus of "Oh, I don't know about the orange one!" However, at the last minute, when it was the one I chose, everyone knew it was perfect.

The fun part of awards shows is getting ready. I have worked with the same glam squad forever. My stylist, sweet, eccentric,

Jessica Paster, has great taste, always picks the right outfit, and makes me piss myself laughing. Robert Ramos, hair, and makeup artist Colleen Campbell-Olwell are so kind, loving, and great at what they do. And because I love them all, that becomes the fun part, hanging out with them.

Most of the rest of it, I could take or leave. I approach events like a job. I know I can do them well. I don't mind talking to the press or promoting something I'm proud of, but I always feel self-conscious about all the attention. Getting my picture taken, over and over. And then, because I don't drink, I get bored easily at any events held after the main one, so I don't like to linger. I have gotten better at it over the years and even learned to find some enjoyment in it. The older I get, the more appreciative I am. Of everything. And that includes awards shows and their after-parties.

I loved the Golden Globes in 2011, the year I was nominated for my role as Gemma on *Sons of Anarchy*. I was so proud of my work on that show, and the nomination felt like recognition not only for me but also for the great writing that made that character who she was. My husband, Kurt Sutter, wrote her, created that world, and so that shout-out felt like it was for him as much as for me.

One of my favorite pictures ever is from that night: Kurt and Sarah and Jackson and me. We took the big kids that year (Esmé was too little), which made it feel all the more exciting. They got glam-squadded by my fine folks as well. Jess dressed Sarah, and Robert and Colleen did her up. And a new suit for Jackson. They sat way up in the nosebleeds, and Kurt and I sat down at the tables with the TV people. At the Golden Globes, the movie stars are at the center tables, and then TV people are on the periphery, so that's where Kurt and I were. We were squished into this teeny-weeny table with FX network president John Landgraf and his wife, actress Ally Walker, my *SOA* costar that year. As my category came up, Ally started whispering to me, "You're going to win. I can feel it. You're going to win."

"No, Ally, I'm not," I whispered back. "I never do."

And then, I did.

For the dramatic turn I'd wanted to make.

For the work I'd known (hoped) I could pull off.

After so many years of being labeled "comedic," to win Best Performance by an Actress in a Television Series—Drama was confirmation that I'd scaled a major hurdle. And as Kurt had always intended, "We had finally killed Mrs. Bundy."

I felt proud.

We went to the party afterward. I walked around barefoot because I couldn't bear wearing my high heels anymore. My feet hurt. And everyone loosens up at those things. Lots of bare feet and tummies no longer sucked in. The magical part about winning is that, if you have a globe award in hand, you can talk to anyone, and everyone wants to talk to you. Sarah wanted to meet British actor Colin Firth, so we did. Dame Helen Mirren talked to me like we were old friends, even though we'd never, ever met. Anne Hathaway chased me down and leapt into my arms, letting me know how happy she was to see me. She also reminded me of a kindness I'd paid her during her performance in her first film.

But, truthfully, that night was an anomaly. Normally, even though I've had this crazy, wild job for most of my adult life, I'm still not used to, or comfortable with, those supposedly glamorous aspects of it. I usually skip the accoutrements. Whenever possible.

Fame and celebrity have come up as something for me to share in this book, and so I reflect on them. But weeding through my complicated feelings has been really difficult. I've started to write this chapter, and then rewrite this chapter, time and again. It got to the point where I'd do anything to not sit down and write it. Even cleaning my youngest's play area. Although it wasn't my intention. It wasn't my plan. It wasn't on my to-do list. But while taking my damn computer out of its case, I had an urge to tackle that niggly job rather than the commitment I'd made to myself to write about my conflicted feelings about fame. So I wiped down the swing set, easel, plastic plates, and wooden fruit that live in her dollhouse kitchen. Kaboomed the spiderwebs and wet mopped the dollhouse floor and tried not to think about what I wasn't doing. Because it freaked me out.

Finally, I faced down what had been making me uncomfortable.

To complain about fame makes me sound like I'm a pompous ass: "Oh, poor me, I have to get dressed up and be fawned over."

Of course, I didn't get on this bus to *not* be noticed. But it was never my dream to be famous. I wanted the respect of my peers and to be able to support myself as an artist. The path I'm on has always rang a bigger bell than fame. It was about doing what I was good at. It's the only path I could take. I wasn't good at anything else. I wasn't a good student. I wasn't good at making friends. My only skill set was expression.

My friend Johnny Segal, who I went to high school with, and who saw how I was comfortable in my skin only when I was performing, used to say I was "famous" long before I was famous. I think what he meant was that my path was clear—not always clear in the forms it would take, but that my voice was loud and needed to be expressed. He meant that I was meant to be seen and heard.

And along with that, famous.

Fame and celebrity are not what holds my attention. It is my least favorite part of what I do—though I'm quick to admit it does come with some special perks I'm quite keen on: a table without a reservation, or a seat moved on an airplane by an enamored flight attendant.

But I struggle with it.

I am embarrassed by it yet arrogantly prideful about it at the same time.

I have a constant nagging need to be noticed, yet I also want to know "What the fuck are *you* looking at?"

And truthfully, I don't fully grasp that I'm famous.

It's hard to think that anybody might give a shit about what I have to say.

After all, I'm famous. But not "Jane Fonda famous."

Now, *she's* somebody whose every word I hang on.

Everything about her: from her early years as an insecure Hollywood starlet to her struggles with anorexia and romances with distant men (like her dad) and continuing to be sexual into her seventies, she's awesome, and I'm fascinated.

Me, well, there is meaning to the work and things I've done. But I never started an exercise revolution. I never became controversial because of my political beliefs. I don't believe I've affected change on a grand scale. I think I make a contribution. I know I've made people laugh. Through characters I have played, I've certainly allowed people to access their own expression of sadness or remorse, anger or disappointment. I've always believed that being an actor is a great service job. And I am of service.

But it's just a job.

So much of the glitz and fame, I can't even remember. I have blank spots where spotlights have been. It's easier for me to remember the ordinary goings-on of my life, because that's what my life is most of the time.

It's just a life.

Mine, like yours, has moaned and groaned.

Stretched and turned.

Sometimes good, oftentimes bad.

People up and gone, love found and thrown away.

Many moments make up a life.

I am surprised by how many of my fame moments are blank spots.

The volume turned down.

Fame wants to turn up the volume on everything. It wears me out and intrudes on my need for solitude. And right when fame first came into my life was also when I was first getting sober. To stay sober, I had to adopt a central tenant of the rooms, which was all about "staying right-sized": not standing out, just being happy and healthy in the middle of the herd. I loved the anonymity of that.

I can remember the glory moments of my career if reminded, but they have always seemed more memorable and impressive to other people that may have shared them with me or observed them. The night of my Golden Globe win, maybe having grown, I could really be there and absorb it as it was happening. I was proud, and I could see how fun and rare and exciting the night was for Sarah and Jackson, and living it through their experience imbued it with more of those positives for me than it would have possessed in the past. There was a day, I would have experienced and remembered only the dress and not the rest of it.

I know people who have their lives stored neatly, well organized, in their brains. Able to rattle off stories and lessons learned in Technicolor detail, in chronological order, no big deal, without the slightest bit of haze.

Not so in my case. I've always been fuzzy.

My furrowed brow and blank stare in the face of facts that should fill me up with emotion at their memory has been curious to me. It made me wonder, *Where have I been for so much of my life?*

I was always floating above events. Never sitting in the middle of them. Like it wasn't really me showing up on sets, sitting for hours in hair and makeup, week after week, going to table reads, camera blocking on Wednesdays, shooting two shows on a Friday night in front of a studio audience, learning lines, hitting marks, going to premieres, being on magazine covers, getting nominations.

It *was* me, yes.

I just think I missed a lot.

Struggling in my duality.

Embarrassed of and at the same time enamored of all the attention.

That old *kina hora* mind-set I inherited from my father, where you don't fully acknowledge good things, for fear they'll be taken away. And also, because I grew up around Hollywood, and my dad's approach was always so hardworking and practical. Not glamorous at all.

Maybe because of all that, it seems ordinary to me. Not extraordinary.

But I'm told it is not . . . ordinary.

At first, I couldn't accept success as an actor. I always thought it was the wrong job for me. I spent so many years struggling for employment and respect as a musician, I found it really hard to get comfortable as an actor and accept the recognition it started to bring. It just wasn't the picture I had for myself.

I also always had a raucous, colorful, often traumatic, personal life going on simultaneously behind the scenes of my professional life. That also contributed to pulling my focus from where I was. First, there was early sobriety, requiring a total redo of all I'd done before. Then, dating in early sobriety (awkward and terrifying), doing everything for the first time sober. Being in the public eye, suddenly famous at thirty-three while inside feeling like I was still the gawky fifteen-year-old with escape on her mind. All these feelings and fears colliding within me, I kept to myself when I was at work. And I definitely didn't want to be around other people—or in the spotlight—outside of work. It weirdly mimicked how my life had always felt, my insides never matching up with my outsides, and feeling like I could never tell the tale.

I guess you could say I was still living the personal life of a musician more than the personal life of an actress, which I viewed as being a bit tamer than how I was living, even sober. If my rock star dreams had come true, my home life—eventually married to a rock star drummer; a social life fraught with ex-junkies and alcoholics—would have seemed like the norm compared with my peers. As it was, my home life never felt like what might be going on in my coworkers' lives.

I felt like I was kind of in the wrong place, and life was just pushing me along while I was thinking, *Wait a minute, wait a minute.* And it was that distance between where I was and where I thought I should be that led to the out-of-body feeling and my missing all those moments.

It didn't help that my musical dreams always seemed to still be within reach and kept pulling me out of where I was. All the years I was on *Married with Children*, I continued to have a band. Five years in, I got a label deal and in 1994 released an album, *Well . . .* , on Virgin Records. The company signed me based on my legitimacy as a musician, not on my television notoriety.

I made sure to write or cowrite all the songs on that album. I adamantly insisted on being taken seriously as a songwriter and not being seen as a TV celebrity trying to cash in with a vanity project. My music was not that. It was sincere.

I made a good record. It was well reviewed. I was proud to promote it.

I went on a national tour to radio stations to do meet-and-greets and promote *Well* . . . It got a few minutes of airtime wherever I went, but interviews inevitably ended with talk of Peg, the outrageousness of *MWC*, and a request for Peg's signature phrase: "Oh, Al." Folks really wanted to talk only about Peg Bundy.

These days, it's a lot easier for actors to cross over into careers in music and for musicians to cross over into acting, but at that time, it was really difficult to be taken seriously if you jumped from one to the other.

So here I was, five years into doing the job I wasn't sure I was meant for, finally landing another record deal, finally getting another shot at the job I'd always wanted to do. And my accomplishment lacked the validity—the affirmation—I'd longed for. My music wasn't taken seriously. Which was a shock to everybody, really. The record company, too.

"This is so good," everyone in the know said.

But it didn't matter.

I was now Peg Bundy to the world.

No wonder I had such a conflicted relationship with my fame.

Particularly at that time, and particularly fame earned in that way.

When you're on television, people come up to you on the street. If you're in the movies, people stand back. It's that thing of being in people's living rooms. They think they know you.

And they want you to be the person they have come to know and love. They think they can say anything to you. (And remember, I'm the person who got anxiety going on a date—fuck that, even getting dressed for a date!—without a drink.) Maybe that's the part that needles me with discomfort: the intrusion, the part that makes me think, *What the fuck are you looking at?*

I'm not Jane Fonda famous.

I'm just on TV.

No Longer a Fraud

So now I am an actress.

Against my will, almost.

What does that feel like?

It took me years of being on television before I felt I belonged there. While there, I studied. I coached. I learned on the job. I acted as if I knew what I was doing.

When Danny DeVito directed me in my first TV role on the *Mary* show, he had to explain what it meant to "hit your mark."

Mary Tyler Moore used to lift my chin and say, "Find your light. Try to feel it."

I had no clue what she meant.

And I started out as a comedic actress, which was always a weird concept to me, as I've never thought of myself as very funny. I do have timing. Comedy is about time. But if you ask anyone in my family, they would never say, "She's the funny one." More like "the overdramatic, sensitive one." I've used sarcasm to cover and protect my fragile feelings. Sarcasm has always been my default. My contribution to conversation. My worldview. That translates into "funny," I suppose, but more of a sneaky, dark aside than a barrage of hilarious jokes.

When *Married with Children* came to be, it was an era when stand-up comedians were all the rage. Every network was on the hunt for a stand-up's point of view around which to build a show. Roseanne Barr, Brett Butler, Bill Cosby—I was not that. I cannot make something funny if it's not written that way. I can enhance, add character, but I'm not a good joke/storyteller. Although humor is born of painful experience, mine never translated for me as good material for folly. I was always more about the blues than the funny.

So as much as I loved playing Peg Bundy, and as much as I ultimately felt confident in the role, I never felt that comedy was my long game as an actress. The longer I played in that format, the more I wanted to work my more overemotional dramatic chops. I longed to find roles that served them. I believed that was really the truth of myself as an actor.

After eleven years in that flamboyant red wig, capri pants, and mules, not everybody saw my vision as clearly as I did or hoped they would. The idea was unproven and not marketable in the eyes of possible employers to see "Peg Bundy" as anything but her.

It's the double-edged sword of a success that brings you into people's living rooms for so many years, so much so that they start to believe what they see on their TV every week is who you really are. They are uncomfortable and suspicious of any change, betrayed somehow by the actress stepping out from behind the persona of the character they now think of as a friend or relative. They like laughing, and they don't want to lose her in that role.

Trying to land a serious part was not dissimilar from when I released my first solo record while on *MWC*, and it was never taken seriously. The face of Peg Bundy was hard to shake. Of course, I was grateful for the work, the success, the high ride. But now, at the end of the ride, I was left confused and unmotivated by the bag I was stuck in. The bag that wanted me to do only more of the same.

I knew I was a dramatic actress.

But nobody else did.

Married with Children ended in 1997, and the next three years were a time of intermittent employment. I had a development deal at CBS, but we never found the right project. I shot a pilot for ABC, *Earth Scum*, a comedy about an earthling (me) married to an alien, played by Mark Addy, that I loved but that never saw the light of day. In 2000 came a sitcom for NBC, *Tucker*, which started out strong and then limped to the end of its thirteen-episode order. Two years later, I costarred in a series with Hank Azaria, *Imagine That*, only to have him lose faith in it halfway through our thirteen-episode order, and—truly artistic dude that he is—just end it! Imagine *that*. All comedies.

I was working, but it was eye opening on so many levels. I had naïvely believed that a successful run on a TV show was easy to come by and that dramatic roles would easily open up to me as well. With *Married with Children* having been only my second shot up to bat, I thought it would always be like that. I was also shocked at how shortsighted creatives were. Folks actually thought I looked like Peg Bundy. That I *was* Peg Bundy! How many general interviews I had to take just to prove I wasn't a spandex-wearing redhead. I was sure to dress just the opposite. I quickly eliminated any red hair from my head. I did not wear anything too tight or too sexy. But even in jeans and a T-shirt, they saw me as Peg.

The shift came slowly. Two years after *MWC* ended, I entered the world of voice acting as Leela on *Futurama*, a Matt Groening and David X. Cohen–created cult favorite also on FOX. As I remember, Matt and I, as early residents of this new network, had become friendly after attending many events together. He brought me in to read for his new show and hired me. Cast alongside an incredible array of voice actors—Billy West, John DiMaggio, Tress MacNeille, Maurice LaMarche, Phil LaMarr, Lauren Tom, and David Herman—I once again was learning on the job. Though exciting and hysterically funny, I was yet to fulfill my drama dreams.

In 2000 I auditioned for *8 Simple Rules*, to play the role of the wife of the most amazing person, John Ritter. It was a comedy, but much more reality based than the ones I had been considered for in the recent past. Getting that gig was no easy feat. My bellwether, Belle, had to work her magic, bang down doors, *insist* that I be seen for the role. The network was not high on me. The producers were skeptical. They were nervous that together John (also known for playing an iconic comedy role, Jack Tripper on

Three's Company) and I would not be taken as anything other than "Jack" and "Peg."

So I went in to read with John. We had worked together previously, playing love interests in a very forgettable TV movie in which he fell for my character, his overweight best friend. (I had to wear a fat suit in the movie. Really! They padded me!) We'd had a good bonding experience. He was a hard guy not to love immediately. Warm, endearing, and pee-in-your-pants funny. Oddly, we had been on set together the night it was reported that Princess Diana had been killed, in 1997. We sat in my trailer together, having just met—strangers, really. Wanting to share the experience with someone, we watched that most heartbreaking moment together.

Years later, when I read that he was doing a new sitcom, I wanted to be in it. I didn't even need to read it. I didn't care what it was. I just wanted to work with John. When I finally got an audition, he was there. There were three other actresses reading with him for the role as well. John lit up when he saw me in the waiting room.

Taking me aside, he whispered in my ear, "I want you for the part. You are my number one choice. I got your back."

Network auditions suck. No matter how prepared you are, nerves are relentless, mouth dries up, lines you know you know fade from your brain.

It sucks.

The only hope of getting through them is to become present with the character. Forget that anyone else is in the room other than the other actor you are with, forget that you are being judged, forget about the contract you just had to sign for the amount of time you will have a job and the money you will be paid—if you get the role. They do this all beforehand, before you even open your mouth, betting on the outcome. You have to forget about the other actors in the waiting room, whom you instantly assume will do a better job than you. Either that, or just the opposite: upon seeing them, you somehow solidly know *I got this!* Just forget it all and be in the moment of the scene you are doing.

And that sweet John Ritter—that great, giving actor—created the moment, and I went right there with him. It was just us in the room, and we were calm, believable, funny with the chemistry of a longtime married couple.

I got the job.

I was not goofy, eccentric, cartoonish, or over the top in my role as Cate Hennessy. She was grounded and physically looked more like me than the characters I had played previously. It was a small crack in the opening of me exploring myself as a more dramatic actress.

In a most ironic and heart-wrenching twist, though, my role on *8 Simple Rules* became, for a brief time, a truly dramatic one. The show had been enormously well received the first season. High ratings, People's Choice Award, a growing success, and we'd only just begun. We had just returned to begin shooting our second season when the worst tragedy of my working life befell our lovely success.

John Ritter died.

At around four o'clock on September 11, 2003, out of nowhere, John complained of not feeling well, a bit nauseous, and said he needed to lie down. He was rushed to the hospital, and then, shockingly, pronounced dead at ten that night. Doctors initially suspected that he'd suffered a heart attack. They determined too late that, in fact, his aorta, the largest blood vessel in the body, had ruptured. He was just fifty-four, had a five-year-old daughter from his second marriage, and three other children from his first marriage.

I can speak here of how much I loved him. Of his angelic spirit, coupled with his deep, dark soul. A darkness he hid well, but I had spied. Or maybe he'd let me in on. Or most likely, I'd felt kindred to because of my own dark places.

Working on any kind of production, the tone of the working environment is always set by whoever is in the "top dog" position. Number one on the call sheet. If that position is filled by an inconsiderate, selfish prick, all the relationships on set will suffer, and whining, complaining, and pettiness will ensue. Our number one on *8SR* was John. And the tone he set was love.

Just the right combination of laughter and professionalism, the workday was filled with his *insanely brilliant* sense of humor, just enough practical joking to keep the energy high, and a committed work ethic, so the end product appeared effortless yet precise. He was a comedic master and an angel. I've never met anyone like John, and I feel him around me, still, in my life. So, really, no shit, an angel.

The network and the show's writers and producers decided to keep *8 Simple Rules* on the air after John passed and to play out the death of the family's patriarch. This was partially a financial decision. But also a very emotional one. Ending right after the abruptness of John's passing felt too jarring emotionally for all involved. His real-life family as well. It was a bold move in a comedic arena, yet the only one that felt appropriate.

So we stayed with that story line. The Hennessys lost the head of their household, just as we had lost the head of our little make-believe family. So brokenhearted were we all at losing our John, our real emotional lives—mine, as well as those of the three actors playing our kids, Kaley Cuoco, Amy Davidson, and Martin Spanjers—overrode any acting that was required to play those scenes of realization. The show took on a dramatic tone, and my performance called for no acting at all.

Dad had died.

John had died.

Lines were blurred.

The network was anxious to get *8 Simple Rules* back to funny. The now-hybrid nature of our show, which was supposed to be a comedy but now had a serious subject to tackle, was just too risky to really let play out for as long as it actually should have.

The truthful healing of a family.

A now-single working mom.

Jim Garner was brought in to play my soulful father, who moved in to help the family—a role he filled beautifully, I might add. But he didn't do much for the comedic edge the network wanted to return to. Within four airings, David Spade was cast as cousin C.J. Barnes to lighten the dramatic load and bring back some funny. But we never quite regained our stride.

8 Simple Rules ended after three seasons.

Thankfully for my career, that same year *Lost* was casting for the girlfriend of John Locke (Terry O'Quinn). A recurring dramatic role on one of my favorite shows at the time. Belle and I tossed my hat into the ring, and I was asked to come in and audition. Once again, I needed to reassure and prove to all creatives involved that I could handle a dramatic turn.

I read twice.

They needed to be *really* sure.

I got the job, and Helen Norwood became another piece of that iconic TV show's lore, as the star-crossed lover of John Locke, one of the victims of the plane crash that set up the show. After he finally returned from the island, he discovered that she had died of a brain aneurism. I changed my look for that role. (I love to do that.) I went blonde. She was feminine, in a soft, lovely way. The role added another notch in my dramatic actress belt. I came to find out that *Lost*'s executive producer–director, Jack Bender, who'd been John Ritter's best friend, had been my behind-the-scenes champion all along. Apparently John continued to have my back, just like he always had in life.

The final nail in the Peg Bundy coffin (I joke: I love her, but she was limiting me. I needed her to step back and let me see what I could do as an actress!) came in the form of a part written specifically for me by my husband, Kurt Sutter. He was finishing up his time on *The Shield*, the award-winning crime drama he had been with for its entire seven-year run, working his way up from story editor to executive producer. He was now in search of his "what's next" and was pitched the idea of a show that takes place among outlaw motorcycle clubs. He sparked to that world, and spun a bare-bones idea into *Sons of Anarchy*. He came to me and said he was writing a part for me. Originally, this was to be a secondary role—the mother of his lead character—in what he was imagining as a testosterone-heavy drama.

"Would you be interested?" he asked. Kurt understood my desire to take on more dramatic roles. He also believed I had the chops and just needed a break to move into such roles. I was thrilled. Not only for the support he was throwing my way but also for the opportunity to work with such a great storyteller. Over the years, I'd read all of Kurt's scripts—every episode of *The Shield* he'd written, every development step of every feature film he'd created or rewrote. I knew how talented he was.

He fancied me his muse. His "good-luck charm."

I would have said yes to anything he wanted to write for me. As it turned out, Gemma Teller became one of the strongest female roles created in that newly expanding cable television landscape. The show eventually landed at FX. Upon reading the first draft, I hoped the network would approve me in the role of matriarch. And it not only approved but also asked Kurt to expand the role and enhance the mother-son relationship. *Sons of Anarchy* morphed into an emotional family drama set in a world few knew much about. And it went on to become one of the highest-rated cable shows in history. Week after week, beating the major network numbers.

Creatively, it was a dream role. I'm certain there will never be another like it. Good writing is rare. Kick-ass female characters, though more common in recent years, are still rare. Gemma was so different from me and yet maternal like me, which made her fascinating to play. Her instincts were like mine, but her actions were so different from anything I would ever do. I got to take so many risks. My character was put in a lot of positions that stretched me as an actor, and, just like my first role on television, I always felt like I was learning on the job. I couldn't cruise. It always felt like I was facing a new challenge, something I hadn't done yet, which was so invigorating and made every day at work so great.

As an artistic person, you want to remain interested in what you're making, and to do so, you have to jump off a cliff again and again. Kurt's writing really provided me with that opportunity.

On that job, for the first time in my long and varied career, I never felt like a fraud. Finally, this was the role that made me feel like I was an actor.

My Number

I'm working on my book in every coffee shop from Hollywood to the Westside of LA, daily, agonizingly. I get distracted and watch the people around me. There, across the coffee cups, amid the smell of espresso, sit a man and a woman, who I definitely think are father and daughter.

And suddenly, they are sucking face, and I'm frozen in disbelief.

He's got a good thirty years on her.

She's hot.

He's not even okay.

This isn't the first time I've seen this.

Is it a trend?

It's definitely something.

I see such moments regularly enough to feel the uncomfortable reality of our culture reflecting back onto me. I imagine "youth" stealing my jobs, my man, my brain, my place in the world. All because I've lived longer, and that alters what people see when they look at me. Or whether they see me at all.

Young packaging is appealing. And sought after.

I grew up in California. Land of youth, suntans, and movie stars. Getting older is something to hide. On the sets where my dad was a TV director, making art the Hollywood way. In my house, where if the houseplants got wilty, my mother threw them away. God forbid my father should see them.

"Why are these dying plants here?" he would have said.

So Mom served as our home's set director, tossing out the plants rather than watering them.

Everything had to be young and fresh; not old or saggy or brittle or faded. That was what I thought my father was saying: in a perfect world, nothing ages.

So, true to form, my parents didn't either.

They just died.

Now, where did that leave me, well into my own adulthood, staring down the barrel of a big birthday my parents had never lived to see? It left me feeling self-conscious and uncomfortable, both invisible and a flagrant affront all at once.

It was January 19, 2014, and the air was crisp, and cool for LA. I had left my house early to have some alone time to make myself calm and beautiful, checking into a room at the Palihouse hotel so I could change into my party dress. I'd never thrown a party for myself before, and I was clammy. I'd been at a loss as to what to wear. So I'd asked my friend and stylist, Jessica, who had styled me for many events, if she would lend me an outfit. Together we picked out a very formfitting, sexy blue dress. The day I tried it on at Jessica's house, it had looked really good.

But now, when I put it on, I couldn't face myself in the mirror. If I did, I knew my usual distorted vision of myself would take over. And so I did what I've learned to do with the wisdom of years: never look in mirrors for very long. Instead, I trusted that the dress looked good, because Jessica said it did and because it had looked good at her house. I knew to take my focus off what I looked like and just get out the door. I felt sexy, sure, but if I stared too hard at myself, that could all change.

Downstairs in the lobby of the very understated, expensively retro, hip Hollywood hotel, my best friend, manager, and long-time bellwether, Belle, was waiting for the guests to arrive. With her at the evening's helm, doing what she does so well, I knew I could relax—as much as possible.

My husband, Kurt, and my lanky, warmhearted son, Jackson, came up to the hotel room early to make sure that I actually went to my own party. When they arrived, Jackson, my puppy son, who we refer to in our family as "the boy," bounded into the room.

Kurt has a very good sense of when it's time to wear a suit, and he had put one on that night. He looked great, with his tattoos peeking out beneath the cuffs of his jacket, and all of his bracelets and rings. I love how Kurt looks. When he walked in, he made my heart flutter.

"Hey, Mom, this is going to be such a cool night," Jackson said. "Phoebe's downstairs, we've got our guitars, the band is setting up. This place is so fucking cool."

One of the things I love so much about Jackson is his enthusiasm. It's contagious. His joy for the moment made me feel like it was safe to be excited too.

Walking on either side, my two guys escorted me toward the hotel elevator.

It was nice to feel so supported by my current marriage and my son, the most consistent men I've ever had in my life.

The party was in the lounge-like lobby. As we reached the cusp of the action, Kurt and Jackson looked at me, and without a word, I stopped in my tracks, tilted my head, and listened. There was a clink of glasses, a hum of voices, the anticipation of my arrival—the hair on my arms raised, my breath caught in my throat, my armpits glowed.

I was having a party for a big birthday.

A milestone.

And I wasn't sure I wanted to go.

I held back for a moment, breathing deep, soaking in the room's cool elegance. I was trying to make myself ready to be seen by everyone from every stage of my life, all of whom I'd chosen to gather together. They were all here to share in this incredible, uncomfortable, big moment with me.

In the weeks leading up to the party, I'd been thinking a lot about the milestone. As much as I tried to deny that I cared, I couldn't close my eyes to my number. Reaching the end of a decade, the start of another, made me feel anxious, unsettled, and full of questions about what the fuck happens now.

So I decided to start the new year by celebrating. Planning it would help. I threw myself this birthday party, believing that this would be the last birthday I'd acknowledge. I did it up big. I made it sound like Belle and my husband threw my party for me, but really, it was my instigation. It was a gift to myself, and in so doing, I took full responsibility that at the end of the day, I would never do it again!

It wasn't the party's fault.

That was lovely.

Friends, family, history.

Hip locale, great food, jazz band.

Here's the problem: I thought that celebrating my landmark age would allow me an easier transition into accepting it. I was wrong.

Here's my advice: if you're uncomfortable with getting older, don't shine a light on it. In fact, start counting fucking backward. Live by "A lady never tells her age," even if you're a guy.

Something really shifted in the way I thought about myself when I came smack up against my number.

Yeah, some good stuff. I'm wiser. I don't give a fuck what other people think. (That's not quite true: I am afraid you'll think I'm old!) I am more spiritually prioritized. All good stuff.

I've always looked young for my age, too. I'd say at this one, I looked in my midforties. Inside I felt sprung and seriously fuck-able. So it was a confusing day, as dreadful as I'd dreaded it would be. I felt as young as I looked, but I worried others wouldn't see me that way. Or even worse, they wouldn't see me at all, or they'd see how much I cared about how they saw me. I hated finding myself here just because I'd lived another year. I knew I should be grateful to be alive. And I was. But . . . *fuck*.

Because, as that birthday arrived, I suddenly questioned "my feminine self." I should say, "my sexy feminine self." I had been called in the press everything from the "original MILF" to "a badass biker bitch." Since I'm only intermittently aware of my sex appeal, and since I realized it later than most, I wasn't ready to be cast out yet.

Just like that, with the turning of one year into the next, I imagined that the world had stopped seeing me as "sexy." Or that it had stopped seeing me at all. As if overnight, I'd disappeared. Yet there I was, celebrating, while at the same time feeling I might be done. And now, because of my own decision to bring everyone together, I had witnesses to my folly.

Everyone looked good in the dimly lit lobby/bar/living room vibe of the Palihouse, with its vintage velvet couches, potted succulents, and stacks of hardcover books scattered amid the curated careless decor.

The faces of friends, old and new.

My junior high school friend Debbie Gasster, still blondish, wearing her same warm smile that reminded me of her mother— the only June Cleaver type from my early, chaotic life. Debbie, who'd flown in from Oregon, is the person I've known the longest.

On the dance floor, Allison Janney danced with the equally statuesque Ally Walker, my *Sons of Anarchy*'s character's foe, whom I fell in love with on the set and became very close to. Allison, the welcomed guest, once again showing up at my party with one mutual friend or another. It's now our little joke, because we barely know each other, but there we are, always at each other's parties, dancing, celebrating. Besides, who the fuck really knows anybody anyway?

Sitting at a table on the edge of the dance floor, some newer friends. My friend Drea de Matteo, celebrating her own birthday that day, deep in conversation with Marilyn Manson. (Or maybe she was just listening; he likes to chat!) My *Sons of Anarchy* family: a very pregnant Maggie Siff, Mark Boone Junior, Dayton Callie, Michael Ornstein, and Jeff Kober and his fabulous wife, my close friend Adele Slaughter.

Midway through the party, Jackson reached for his guitar. His bandmate, blonde, brown-eyed Phoebe Bridgers close behind, her guitar also in hand. They hushed the jazz band and stepped up to the mic. The room fell silent but for the bartenders handing out drinks, and a few stray conversations not yet ended. Phoebe and Jackson had a surprise for me.

Jackson scrunched his hair, as he always does, leaving one eye free to look out at the crowd, part Elvis, part his dad, in all of his nineteen-year-old gorgeousness.

"I have a song to sing for my mom," he said, speaking softly, as if it were just us.

"Mom, could you come up close?"

My heart filled with love for my only boy. I felt myself glide to the front of the room. Maybe being this age wasn't *so* bad. There are benefits.

I stood facing them.

Jackson counted off, "One, two, three . . ." and they began to play. The melody materialized, and I realized they were playing a familiar tune. One I wrote, years ago, called "Daddy's Girl." I'd never heard them play it before, and they put their own spin on it. It filled me up. The kindness of the gesture. Jackson giving me back a piece of myself; a vision of who I was so many years ago:

> *My old man,*
> *I'm a chip off the old block.*
> *My old man*
> *Is still living here.*
> *Not in flesh and bone, he's never far from home.*
> *I'm forever walkin' in my daddy's shoes.*
> *I've got his misery, I got good company.*
> *Guess I'll always be*
> *my daddy's girl.*

The song took me back to my twenties. (That's what happens with big birthdays: sideswiped!) It was poetry that half the room was filled with people who knew me when I'd co-written that song with the talented Mark Goldenberg of Cretones fame. Mindy Sterling, my songwriter friend from back in the Laurel Canyon days, when we were the singing duo Sterling Silver; Paul Gordon and Jay Gruska, who wrote the rock musical *Backstreet*, which had just enough rock in it to coax me into trying to act when it was staged at a small theater, setting off my whole career; Debra Dobkin and Jennifer Condos, two of the best sister musicians, whom I'd been lucky enough to play with for years; singer

Sarah Taylor. In our twenties, we were all struggling singers and writers together back in Hollywood. We played music together. We yearned to be heard, in a big way. We were gonna make it. And we all did, in our own ways, although mostly not in the ways we had envisioned.

In walked Bette Midler with husband Martin von Haselberg, a little late, but right on time. My friend Robert Ramos told me she would show up. I hadn't expected her to. We'd had only intermittent contact over the years since I'd sung in her band, but I knew she was in town, so we sent the invitation. Bette has always had a soft spot for me, as I do for her, so I wasn't really surprised she showed.

Twinkling in her practical way, Bette held my face in her hands and looked me in the eyes and didn't need to say a word. Leaving the Divine at home and bringing her real self, which was always the divine I've loved.

A great birthday gift.

I am a girl with a lot of riches. For someone who came of age amid loss after loss, it's remarkable to stand back now and count my blessings. But it can also be disorienting, uncomfortable, just to find myself here. Having lost my mother when she was forty-seven, and my father just five years later, I have no clear concept of aging. My grandparents lived into old age, eighty and beyond, but they lived far away, and after my parents died, I kept my distance. Didn't want to engage. I was young, deep into my addictions, numb to continued familial ties.

Now, outliving and thriving far beyond the hopes and aspirations of my parents . . .

I have no old lady relatives left.

Rose, my dad's mom, made lox and eggs and latkes on Sunday morning. We visited occasionally. She licked a Kleenex to wipe her lipstick off my cheek and spoke only in Yiddish. She always seemed upset. Rose and I were not close.

But Virginia, my mom's mom, and I were close. She was the one who came to stay when Mom would go away. Always coifed, she wore a matching pearl necklace and earrings and had a slow, southern rhythm to her gait. She was practical but feminine, a domesticated career woman. When I was a kid, we were tight, but after my mom died, I drifted. Couldn't keep in touch. I'd like to believe that it was too hard for both of us. My mom was the first of Virginia's four kids to die. Grandma Virginia outlived her second son, my uncle Daniel, as well. Weird.

So no reference point for today.

No awesome role models.

No reason to believe "things get better with age." In fact, quite the opposite.

Here I was, at that "unspeakable" age, surrounded by the friends who had been my extended family until I was of an age to start a family of my own. After Jackson and Phoebe played, my brother, Dave, grabbed the mic and professed his brotherly love and appreciation for his big sis, which made me blush. Paul Reubens, my dorm mate from college, stepped up to give me a toast before dessert. His room at school had looked like Pee-wee's Playhouse, long before there was such a thing. We used to roam the halls of the music department at night and find a piano I could play. He'd sit and listen. He loved to hear me sing, and although

I left college after only one year, we remained close and in touch, mostly his doing.

It's not my nature to stay attached, whereas he's a hugger; he never lets go.

I don't remember his exact toast, but I blushed again and cried at the sentiment.

He said something about my solid, kind, sweet nature . . .

It's always a surprise to me.

Being seen.

I never know how much of myself is visible.

It was a reminder that friends and family see more of me than the exterior I sometimes feel so judged by, in my industry, in my native California—hell, in the world we live in.

My number fucks with me.

I think about it all the time.

Really, it's always on my mind.

I tell myself it doesn't matter. That it's just a number. I don't believe that.

It sounds old.

It sounds gray, and crackly, and saggy.

And not sexy.

That fucks with me. I like being sexy.

Truth is, I'm like a cat on a scratch pole, constantly rubbing up against my husband's leg, his penis, my hand. Constantly horny. I thought that was supposed to all calm down? Right?

Oh fuck, I hate even saying it.

My number.

So I don't.

I cover my gray every two weeks. I stand up extra straight. Always bend from the knees. I walk, I run, I lift, I yoga, I fight, fight, fight getting slumpy, being saggy, drying out. I ruminate with girlfriends about it. We tell ourselves "It's only a number."

But it feels more than that. It feels shameful to me. That's the ugly truth. And taking that one step further, I am threatened by it.

I don't know what to do about any of this. I know to be grateful. I haven't died young. I have survived. And, thankfully, now that the milestone has passed, and I've had a chance to reflect, I have a glimmer of something else. Something beyond.

Something better.

Something sweet and tender.

Wisdom.

It caught me off guard, how my experience could speak, how I could lead by my example, how I could love others by letting them be who they are. So did the realization that I've gained so much more than I've lost because of my number:

The love of my son, Jackson, and my daughters, Sarah and Esmé.

My wonderful Kurt. Husband for keeps.

Even the ones that couldn't stay. My ex Jack, who gave me two of my beautiful children.

And the ones who could and did: all those friends at my milestone party. Everyone seeing me—and accepting me—for who I am. At this number, my number, finally stepping out of discomfort long enough to bask in the gifts that come from being a part of a family of living, loving, wilting humans.

I've Run Away from Home Again

I've run away from home again.

I do it a lot these days . . .

I don't go far, and I am always reachable.

I just stay away from the house.

Not because I don't love my beautiful, Midcentury, extremely awesome house.

It's the activity in it that sometimes . . . I've gotta get away from.

I sink into the cool black leather seats of my car, I turn on the talk radio, I drive with errands to run. I drive with *no* errands to run. I stop for lattes. I eat lunch and check my messages. I try to not text while driving but sometimes can't help it. I soak up the solitude, I replenish.

Life is simpler in my car.

To start with, there are fewer folks onboard.

Fewer as in only me.

I come from a large family, so of course I created a large family so I could feel "right at home."

Truth is, I never felt quite right in the one I came from. As for the one I created, well, as much as I have no regrets, and I love them . . .

I just need a lot of breaks.

I think it's more about me than them, although I am sensitive to high decibel levels, and three kids, three dogs, two birds, fish, and a bearded dragon, and my amazingly colorful husband can really raise the roof at times. I crave silence.

And simplicity.

And it's a habit.

Running away in my car.

It's different now from when I was growing up.

That was more about safety and seeking refuge. Getting my driver's license at sixteen was when I found the golden ticket. I jumped behind the wheel and rarely got out of my car.

I cruised the Sunset Strip.

I roamed the Malibu mountains.

Drove up and down the Pacific Coast Highway, smoking cigarettes (loved them: my best friends), listening to music (no cell phones back then), and making up how I wanted things to be.

It's kind of interesting to think back to before the Internet and the cell phone and the distraction. What was it we were doing?

Sometimes I can remember.

Mostly, time spent in my imagination.

A dying art.

I learned every word to every song on the radio, and I still know them. I can listen back to a Beatles album, or a Neil Young record, and sing along, knowing every word.

Now my brain is mostly in quick-change mode.

I, too, cannot focus very long on one thing at a time anymore.

Always multitasking, like my young-adult children, doing homework while texting while iPodding, with the TV on.

I get it. My brain has been rewired, too.

So, yeah, I've run away today.

Because I still long for the simplicity of solitude.

I run away to find myself. My truest self, the one that's just for me, the one I can only find alone in my car.

Running away reintroduces me to myself.

It reminds me of who I am.

Who I was before my life got big and full.

That's who I still am.

Alone in my car, I'm the me that I've always been.

Famous Last Words

I don't like saying good-bye to anyone after a job ends.

Or the party's over.

I always duck out the back.

I'm not going to say a formal good-bye here, either.

Or wrap it up. Or leave with parting words of wisdom. Or condense what I've learned—or what I'd like to pass on—into a final few meaningful thoughts.

Not going to do that.

I'm in process. As usual.

Just another day.

I've been watching Tony Robbins on Netflix: the documentary *I Am Not Your Guru*.

I stop and start it.

And every time I pick it up, I think, *I'm in love with Tony Robbins.*

I'm *fucking* in love with him, I should say.

He says *fuck*, my favorite expletive, more times than I can count.

Fuck, in all its machinations: fuck, fuck you, motherfucker . . .

I love him.

I love that he looks like a giant.

I love that I believe him when he cries at people's sad stories and hugs them like a bear.

And calls bullshit on that one pretty bitch in the audience who has such high standards for love in her life that no man—let alone the poor schlub she's been holding up to her impossible scrutiny—could ever fucking make her happy.

I love that he stands up for the dude, not the pretty bitches.

I love that he admits to being afraid and does it anyway.

That's exactly how I got here.

It's August 2016.

I've just had lunch with Esmé and sent her off on a playdate and a lizard hunt.

Kurt is away on business for the week.

Sarah and Jackson are both living at home these days, working part-time jobs, figuring out their next moves.

I'm getting my color done this afternoon and wondering when the time will come that I say, "Fuck it, let it go gray!"

And writing my last piece for *Grace Notes*.

Due date has finally arrived.

*   *   *

I started these musings of mine in 2012.

I didn't know then what it was.

Like everything I do, I wanted to keep my writing to myself and share it, both at the same time.

I was flattered when Belle wanted to show it to literary agents, and then when publishers thought my writing was good enough to give me a book deal.

But along the way, I have struggled with the vulnerability that these "notes" of mine have brought up.

Am I brave? Am I egotistical?

I can't believe it will be read.

And . . . I'm so excited it will be read.

I have set myself up for attention, and true to form, I'm not sure I want it.

I don't get angry about my duality these days. I acknowledge it.

Here's what's really good about writing a book when

(a) I wasn't sure I wanted to write one, and

(b) I, for sure, didn't know if I could.

Those thoughts have never gone away, but somehow, in spite of thinking those things, like Tony Robbins, I was scared, but I did it anyway.

Alongside my hesitation, my ambivalence, my fear, my circuitous memory, my boredom with the process, my procrastination.

I wrote shit down, as I'd intended to do, four years ago.

One page at a time.

One word, on one blank page, one after another.

As I do everything.

As I do my job, as I raise my children, as I stay married, as I live sober.

I do it all.

But in small bits.

My credo.

My way through my (most of the time) happy life.

Because from a big, wide worldview, life can overwhelm me.

Still.

When I got sober, I never believed I'd stay that way; it just didn't seem possible.

Thinking about the long haul, for the rest of my life, never again doing what I'd always done to get through the days.

Facing all that and revisiting all that had been, awake, sober, just felt too much for me to walk through.

My life skills unhoned, at thirty-one, still adolescent, I learned how to do what was in front of me.

How to take the next indicated step.

How to stay out of the results.

How to ask for help and follow direction from those with more experience.

I got humble.

And I got well.

It's been thirty years.

And now, the same way that all happened, using those same principles . . .

I wrote a fucking book!

❧ Acknowledgments ❧

I would like to thank everyone who made this book possible, including editor Kate Dresser, publisher Jen Bergstrom, president Louise Burke, copyeditor Philip Bashe, editorial assistant Molly Gregory, and all of the talented team at Gallery Books.

Also thanks to Kirby Kim, Scott Henderson and WME, and Tricia Boczkowski.

Special thanks to Belle Zwerdling and Adele Slaughter, for all your love and teachings.

Special, special thanks to my sweet Sarah Tomlinson.

Also thanks to all the people who keep my day-to-day afloat so I could have time to write this fucking book: Jill Prives, Gloria Echenique, Allie Misuzawa, and Jenita Jones.

Thanks to the Palihouse, my unofficial writing space.

And thanks to everyone along the way to here, both named in this book, and not.

The friends of Bill W.

And always and forever, Kurt, and my kids.

❧ Photo Credits ❧

All photos courtesy of the author, with the exception of the following:

Page 39: Courtesy of Belle Zwerdling

Page 69: From the Mark Taper Forum production of *The Beautiful Lady*; photo by Jay Thompson

Pages 73 and 79: Courtesy of Belle Zwerdling

Page 93: Photo by Norman Seef

Page 101: Courtesy of Johnny Starbuck

Page 111: Courtesy of Belle Zwerdling

Page 119: *Married . . . with Children* © ELP Communications Inc., courtesy of Sony Television Pictures

Page 145: Courtesy of Susan Sherdian Photography

Page 159: Photo by Michael DAmbrosia (MichaelDAmbrosia .com)

Page 201: Todd Williamson Archive/WireImage/Getty Images

Page 213: *Sons of Anarchy* © 2008 Twentieth Century Fox Television. All rights reserved.